NEEDLEWORK
STYLES
FOR
PERIOD
FURNITURE

BOOKS BY HOPE HANLEY

Needlepoint
Needlepoint in America
Needlepoint Rugs
New Methods in Needlepoint
Fun with Needlepoint
The ABCs of Needlepoint
Hope Hanley's Needlepoint Designs
Needlework Styles for Period Furniture

NEEDLEWORK STYLES FOR PERIOD FURNITURE

Hope Hanley

DRAWINGS BY JAMES A. STYGAR
DIAGRAMS BY TRUDY NICHOLSON
CARTOONS BY MARY BETH HAWN
PHOTOGRAPHS (*unless otherwise noted*) BY PHILIP L. COLTRAIN

CHARLES SCRIBNER'S SONS   NEW YORK

Library of Congress Cataloging in Publication Data

Hanley, Hope.
  Needlework styles for period furniture.

  Bibliography: p. 167
  Includes index.
    1. Canvas embroidery—Patterns. 2. Furniture—
History—17th century. 3. Furniture—History—18th
century. 4. Furniture—History—19th century.
I. Title.
TT778.C3H373   746.9'5   78-3496
ISBN 0-684-15582-6

1 3 5 7 9 11 13 15 17 19 MD/C 20 18 16 14 12 10 8 6 4 2

Printed in the United States of America

Acknowledgments

Writing an acknowledgment is difficult because words will not convey the warmth of the gratitude one wishes to express. How does one tell how professional and clever the artists and photographers were, how generous the museum curators were, how helpful one's friends were? My deepest appreciation sounds so trite, a little overblown. Just let it be said that my appreciation is sincere and my gratitude unending.

Mr. and Mrs. Benjamin Ginsburg and Mr. Lewis Rockwell of Benjamin Ginsburg, Antiquary, of New York provided material, suggestions, and education with their usual graciousness. Doris Bowman of the Textile Division of the Smithsonian Institution patiently served as a provider of esoteric information. Elizabeth Ann Coleman, Curator of Textiles and Costume at the Brooklyn Museum, gave generously of her time to find just the material I needed and then some. Trudy Nicholson, who has saved me many a pratfall before, performed again with her usual precision in the diagram department. The same must be said of my daughter, Lee Hanley, who caught her share of mistakes while actually working the patterns.

Friends who readily gave advice and market research are Mrs. Billie Conkling of Billie Conkling Studio, Baltimore, Maryland; the Spauldings at the Elegant Needle, Washington, D.C.; Mrs. Janet Sturtevant of Greengage, Inc., Washington, D.C.; Mrs. Jerry Crute and Mrs. Herme Powell of Jermie's, Richmond, Virginia; Mr. Milton Glaser of Milton Glaser Associates, Richmond, Virginia; Mrs. Augusta Horsey of Art Needlework of Georgia, Atlanta, Georgia; and Mrs. Françoise Woodard and Mrs. Nancy Mrozinski of Washington, D.C. Special thanks must go to my editor, Elinor Parker, who provided me with her usual perceptive advice and judgment.

CONTENTS

To Rocky, in appreciation

NEEDLEWORK STYLES FOR PERIOD FURNITURE

A chair pad made by Ann Marsh of Chester County, Pennsylvania, a needlework teacher who died in 1797. Courtesy of the Chester County Historical Society, West Chester, Pennsylvania. Photo: M. L. Gurtizen.

Foreword

People have beautified their homes with embroidery almost since there have been materials on which to embroider. Bed coverings, bed furnishings, and cushions have been the media for a little self-expression and color. Upholstery of furniture as we know it today, that is, material and padding attached to a wooden frame, did not appear until the sixteenth century. Right from the beginning, needlework was used as an upholstery fabric. There are trends and fashions in embroidery that coincide with the different periods of furniture. In this book these fashions in embroidery and periods of furniture are shown as a guide for those who would like to know "what goes with what."

There are certain kinds of embroidery that are more appropriate for a period of time than others. It is a risky thing to declare that something is not "correct for the period." There is always some museum somewhere that has a perfectly beautiful exception to the rule in its collection. The more embroidery is studied, the greater is the feeling that practically anything goes. Correctness tends to stifle creativity and originality. Unless you are trying to do an authentic restoration, let your taste be the deciding factor on what is correct.

Since most Americans follow derivative French or English decor, these are the areas covered, with an occasional foray into Flemish, Dutch, and Italian influences. This is not meant to be a furniture style book. However, in order to make an informed choice of the appropriate embroidery, you must have some understanding of the style of furniture and its history. You can riffle through the book and find the style of furniture you have and then, ideally, find some indication of what style of embroidery was used on it. Motifs fashionable at the time of the furniture style are listed as well as designers who were influential in setting the style. In this way you can choose motifs that are significant to you and also design your embroidery in the style of the period of your furniture.

Textiles that were used during the same period of time are also mentioned. Perhaps if you don't care for the embroidery style, you might be inspired by the textile designs. There is a precedent for this. Seventeenth-century crewel embroidery designs followed closely the designs of the chintzes from East India. In all of the decorative arts there seems to be a great deal of cross-pollination of ideas. Wallpapers, textiles, embroideries, all seem to follow in one another's footsteps. Occasionally it is possible to discern which one took the lead, but not often.

The important thing is to like your choice of design, whether it is "correct" or not. *You* are going to have to live with it, not the arbiter of what is or is not appropriate to your period of furniture.

CHAPTER ONE

A Bit of Background, Homily, and Other Odds and Ends

In the history of furniture roughly from 1500 to 1900 the countries of Europe took turns setting the trend of fashion. The Italians led off, followed more or less in order by the Flemish, the Dutch, to a lesser extent the Spanish and the Portuguese, and finally the French and English. The latter two, like younger siblings in a large family, had absorbed trends and nuances from those who had gone before, besides originating some distinctive ideas of their own. The French were the leading arbiters from the late seventeenth century on.

The history of upholstered furniture parallels the rise of the merchant class. Heretofore, only royalty had much household furniture and that ran to coffers, chests, and benches, with a bulky wooden chair for the ruler. Starting with the Italian Renaissance, more attention was devoted to the home interior. The merchant ships provided the means for the dissemination of decorating ideas as well as the means to purchase the materials to decorate.

Embroidery, the form of decoration in which we are interested here, enriched churches, castles, and commoners' homes. At first only the richest materials were used—silks, silver and gold threads, even jewels. But as the art of embroidery became more common, so did the materials. This is not to say that fine materials went into total eclipse; the wealthy and royalty still demanded and produced elegant embroidery. Embroidery as an upholstery fabric enjoyed a vogue of three centuries. Then in about 1770 it entered a dry spell, only to emerge again

15

fifty years later in a tidal wave of Berlin work, fancy work, and Art Needlework. This wave lasted until about 1900.

Trying to sort furniture styles into any order is like trying to line up snakes and worms—there are so many twists and turns. It would seem from the titles of books about furniture styles that the English were the orginators of all styles for all of Europe. This is not so. England did evolve some styles, but it was also a melting pot for styles from the Continent. These styles were funneled to America through England and sometimes brought by the colonists themselves directly from the country of origin. Thus English, French, Dutch, and German styles predominate, because these were the predominant nationalities of people who came to America in the seventeenth and eighteenth centuries. English style eventually prevailed because furniture was imported mainly from England until the beginning of our troubles with King George.

To complicate further the classification of American furniture, American craftsmen continued to use furniture styles long after they had become passé in the old country. It usually took fifteen to twenty-five years for the style to catch on in America to begin with. To even further complicate this picture, one will find transitional furniture that combines, for instance, some elements from the Queen Anne style with the Chippendale style. Unless you are an expert, it is difficult to tell exactly where or when a chair was made. Woods give some clues, and some locales made telltale characteristic modifications. It is therefore not easy to assign an embroidery design to a precise period of furniture unless the correct provenance for the furniture is known.

To oversimplify things for the reader not interested in a technical discussion of furniture, there are seven general style periods in America. They are seventeenth century, William and Mary, Queen Anne, Chippendale, Adam-Federal, Empire, and Victorian-Revival. To oversimplify further and aid in identification, it might be said that before the eighteenth century, chair legs had turnings; the eighteenth century brought shape and distinctive feet to the legs; and the nineteenth century is known for its revivals of earlier styles.

During the periods of robust and vigorous furniture styles, such as William and Mary, Queen Anne, and Chippendale, the materials, colors, and patterns of textiles and embroidery were quite bold. During the periods when there was more space than substance in furniture design, the coverings reflected the furniture design. They were lighter and airier, and the colors were more subtle.

Under the heading of inappropriate selections there are only a few style combinations you should try to avoid. Hepplewhite, Sheraton, and Regency chairs do not take to bargello very well. They are too delicate in design themselves to handle the vigorous thrust of pattern. With taste, later periods of the nineteenth century can take bargello, but you must keep in mind the scale of your furniture. Don't ask a dainty damsel from the rococo revival to carry a zebra skin.

Perhaps it is personal prejudice, but nineteenth-century Berlin patterns and eighteenth-century Queen Anne and Chippendale furniture are not a felicitous combination. Wreaths of flowers and large bouquets of full-blown roses are particularly bothersome.

Some nineteenth-century repeat patterns are very hard to distinguish from patterns used in the late eighteenth century; the scale is just a little larger in the earlier ones. Repeat geometric patterns are a good way out of coping with floral designs and their shading if shading is not your strong suit.

An understanding of general textile styles will help in choosing an appropriate design for embroidery. Such a study will prevent you from falling into a historical faux pas, such as using a fabric that had not yet been invented at the time the chair was made. For instance, putting a jacquard-woven fabric on a Chippendale chair would be questionable, since Mr. Jacquard did not invent his loom until early in the nineteenth century.

Conversely, eclectic decor is not new to the history of interior decoration. Americans have been mixing furniture styles since the land was first settled. Necessity was the main reason at first and sentiment later. This is not to say some rooms were not done "en suite," or that some were not right up to date in furniture fashion. But as upholstery wore out, it was replaced with fabric that was in style and available at the time, or with something the lady of the house had made. Thus early eighteenth-century furniture may bear an early nineteenth-century covering. Old nail holes in the chair frame are clues that the current fabric on a chair is not the original one. It is rare to find the original fabric on an old chair. If you are recovering an antique, there is nothing wrong with putting a very modern design on it, if that is what you want. It is just not appropriate to the furniture style. Try to be true to the period of the individual piece of furniture as if it were an entity unto itself. It you don't like the style of needlework for that period, there are alternatives.

One alternative is to imitate the design of the textiles considered appropriate at the time the chair was made. Some designers, Chippendale, for instance, favored a hard-wearing horsehair with a stripe in it for dining-room chairs. This could be imitated in silk and wool. Tapestry is another good source of design as an alternative to needlework designs. The French have been such experts at this practice that one must look closely sometimes to verify whether the covering is needlepoint or tapestry, the designs are so similar.

Chair seat, English, late seventeenth century, design adapted from contemporary damasks. Worked in cross-stitch and half cross-stitch. Courtesy of the Brooklyn Museum, Henry W. Healy Fund.

Then there are always damask patterns. Damask has been made in wool, cotton, and silk. It was not always made in a monochromatic scheme as we know it today but in two or three colors. All you have to do is to find the appropriate damask pattern for your period of furniture.

If you don't want to work needlepoint for your upholstery, there are two other choices: crewel and slipcovers. Slipcases, as they were known then, first became popular during the reign of Louis XIV and were made of elegant materials as well as less elegant ones for summer. Linen and cotton covers were common in eighteenth-century England. They can be seen in satirical prints such as Hogarth's and later in Rowlandson's "Doctor Syntax" series.

Print from the Rowlandson "Doctor Syntax" series. The Reverend Doctor and his cat are resting on a slipcased chair.

Crewel is an obvious choice of technique. Chippendale mentions in some of his correspondence that slipcases were necessary when furniture was covered with needlepoint. Here is a way of having the best of both worlds. Upholster your chair in needlepoint and then make a crewel slipcover. Slipcases in the early eighteenth century were made of chintz or glazed calico; a deep ruffle around the bottom was not unusual. Not only chairs were slipcovered. The *New York Gazette* and the *Weekly Mercury* for August 26, 1776, advertised that Elizabeth Evans " . . . wrought quilts, sopha and settee cases."

Side chair (one of a set of five). Walnut frame, seat and back with slipcovers of needlepoint in wool and silk. Courtesy of the Metropolitan Museum of Art, Collection of Irwin Untermeyer, 1964.

There is some question as to whether crewel upholstery was used in the eighteenth century as much as we are led to believe. There are chairs in existence that bear crewel upholstery obviously made for them, but it was not as typical a material for upholstery as needlepoint or bargello. One of the confusing aspects of the question is that old inventories list crewel upholstery on chairs. One has to decide (unless the chair in question is still in existence) whether the inventory refers to the technique or the kind of wool. Advertisements in old newspapers add clues but no solutions. An advertisement in the *Boston News-Letter* for May 27, 1738, says that Mrs. Condy sold "all sorts of canvas, without drawing; also Silk Shades, Slacks, Floss, Cruells of all sorts. . . ." We know that some bargello coverings and needlepoint too were worked with crewel wools then. Another point to consider is that as crewel-embroidered bed furnishings wore out, it was not unusual to cut out the good parts and use them for something else, then or some years later. This is done even today; lovely old chair frames are reupholstered in yardage from a set of antique bed furnishings.

American wing chair, ca. 1755–1790, made in the Boston area. The silk embroidered upholstery was not made for the chair. It may have been dress material. Courtesy of Historic Deerfield, Inc., Deerfield, Massachusetts.

Other Odds and Ends

In the Colonies bargello was very popular for upholstery for a number of reasons. One is that since the design was not figurative, certain colors—such as green for grass or blue for sky—were not a necessity. It was possible to use whatever colors were at hand. Sometimes colors change in a bargello pattern without warning, indicating that the worker ran out of that color and just went on with another one. Another reason for the popularity of bargello was that an artist

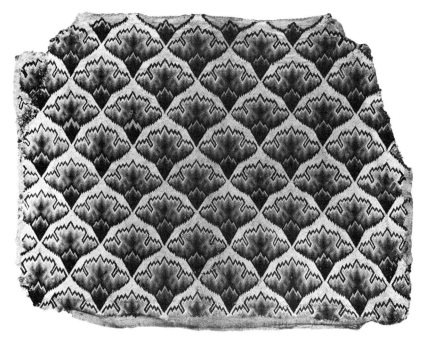

Chair seat, English, eighteenth century, silk and wool on canvas. Victoria and Albert Museum. Crown Copyright.

was not required to apply the design to the canvas. All that was necessary was the canvas or linen and the threads with which to cover it.

There is one big problem in trying to duplicate bargello patterns from the seventeenth and eighteenth centuries—the linen (or hemp) used was much more finely woven than the canvas we use today. If a pattern is repeated literally stitch for stitch, what was only one inch high on the old piece will be four or five inches high on even 14-mesh-to-the-

An adaptation of the Victoria and Albert Museum's eighteenth-century carnation pattern chair seat. Plate 11 illustrates the adaptation mounted on a Chippendale chair. The design has been greatly reduced and simplified. See page 80 for the graphed design. Photo: Philip L. Coltrain.

inch canvas. You have a choice of using very fine canvas and crewel yarn for the original design, or reducing and simplifying the design.

This problem affects figurative designs too. In this case you could use 10/20- or 12/24-mesh canvas and work the detailed parts of the design in petit point and the background in gros point. This is quite authentic to the eighteenth century. The only trouble is that again the canvas used then was finer, so some details must be eliminated or simplified.

If you want to get an idea of scale, sketch your ideas on a sheet of plastic weather sheeting, obtainable at a hardware store, or on a sheet of Dritz tracing cloth for patterns. Use Sharpie markers or crayons. Lay your sketch on the proposed recipient chair. You should be able to see not only the scale but whether or not you like the design on that chair before you commit yourself to canvas or linen.

One of the cardinal rules of needlepoint designing is worth repeating here. Choose your background color *first* and then the color of the subject matter. There are some colors that are more appropriate for certain periods than others and it is important to plan around them. For some periods such as Empire, the backgrounds were very vivid; after 1850 black and very dark colors were used. To experiment with background colors, put sheets of different colors of construction paper under your trial sketch.

In designing Queen Anne or Georgian floral patterns, leave little background. Designs from these periods had very little open background space; a leaf or bud was stuck in, perhaps to avoid doing any more background stitching than was necessary. Outline the leaves and petals either in a light color such as white or beige, or in the palest shade of the color used in the design itself, or in black. Shading is worked from the edge of the petal or leaf in or out, but consistently in or out, and always from the darkest shade to the lightest, petal after petal. Shading was always done in rainbow stripes; no gradual nuances were tried. Realism was not the point.

Perhaps you are planning a figurative scene surrounded with flowers. The center was often done in petit point, and sometimes the flowers in the border were too. The background of the border would be worked in gros point or cross-stitch. Pastoral scenes, so popular in the eighteenth

The floral border of this Queen Anne balloon chair seat intrudes into the scene from John Gray's *Fables,* Kent and Wootton illustrations. English, early eighteenth century, wool and silk on canvas. Victoria and Albert Museum. Crown Copyright.

century, were set in plain ovals with a light outline of another color around them or with a few leaves from the border intruding into the scene. Sometimes they were set in a very simple cartouche.

To use the cartoons in this book, you will have to enlarge them. Measure the area of the chair you wish to cover. Include at least one-half inch on all four sides for the rise of the padding. If you plan to upholster a wing chair in needlework, it would be best to consult with your upholsterer before you start and persuade him to make templates for you. A photographer can photostat a cartoon for a smaller project to your exact measurements; the charge should be under ten dollars. You could enlarge it yourself using a pantograph, but this takes a little practice and for some is never a satisfactory technique.

Another method of enlarging a design is to draw evenly spaced vertical and horizontal lines on a tracing of the cartoon. Count the number of squares created vertically and horizontally, and multiply the two figures one by the other. Multiply the width by the height of the space you wish to cover on your chair. Now divide the smaller figure by the larger chair figure. The result will tell you how many inches apart you must draw the second set of vertical and horizontal lines on

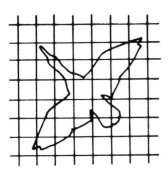

Enlarging a design.

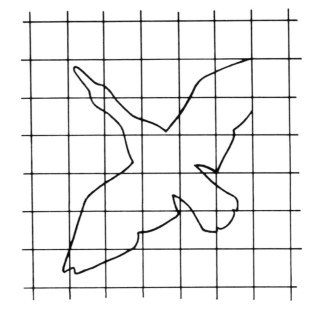

a large piece of tracing paper. If you are an accomplished artist, simply count the number of lines across the tracing and eyeball the same number of lines to fit your space. When your large sheet of crosshatchings is ready, you can start to draw the contents of each small square into the corresponding large square.

When you have finished, outline either your photostat or your self-enlarged cartoon with a felt-tip pen if you are working a needlepoint design. If you are working a crewel design, outline the reverse of your tracing with a Magic Pencil or with Transpaints. The latter will allow you to color an object in the color in which you plan to embroider, the former just in aqua or magenta. When using a transfer pencil or Transpaints, it is a good idea to iron the transfer onto your cloth over a hard surface such as a drawing board.

If you are working in needlepoint, you still have to transfer the enlarged design to your canvas. A glass table on which to lay your cartoon will help a great deal. Set a lamp underneath the table so that the light will help you see the cartoon through the canvas that you will lay over it. If you do not have a glass table, a piece of white paper underneath the cartoon will help. Tack or tape down the cartoon and canvas securely.

Oil paints or acrylics are used for canvas painting. Oil will give a darker-looking product and will take longer to dry. A few drops of Japan dryer in each color will hasten the drying somewhat. Mix the paints just a little thinner than is usual for picture painting. Acrylic paints are brighter and dry in a few hours. They should be mixed to the consistency of cream. Paint as precisely as you can; canvas is not appropriate for a sketchy technique. Make sure only one color is in each intersection of canvas threads. This will make the work easier to stitch. If you must use Magic Markers, test each one before you use it to make sure it really is waterproof. When you are finished, spray the canvas with a clear plastic spray to seal the ink.

The graphed designs in this book were designed with 12- to 14-mesh-per-inch canvas in mind. Remember that graph designs decrease or increase in size depending on the size of canvas mesh used. Some designs included have been vastly reduced from the original examples because they were originally done on fine linen. The carnation design is such an example; the original design worked as is on today's canvas would be seven inches high. Therefore the design was reduced by leaving out some details, but retaining enough to give the original effect. If you want to get the exact proportions of a design scaled to the canvas you plan to use, buy some special needlepoint graph paper in your scale mesh.

Each square on the graph paper represents a stitch for half cross-stitch. For bargello designs each graph line represents a canvas thread. To aid in counting squares on your canvas, crosshatch your canvas with basted running stitches of cotton sewing thread, both vertically and horizontally. For an intricate design you'll need them about every twenty threads, but ordinarily about every fifty threads will do. This is a big help when working bargello. You can see at a glance if you are off the line.

Finally, the choice of your colors is influenced somewhat by the size of canvas you use. A greater contrast in shading is needed for the large-mesh canvases. The finer-mesh canvases have room for more gradations of shading, so more colors and more subtlety can be used.

CHAPTER TWO

Squabs, Cushions, and Early Upholstered Chairs

Oak was the principal wood that joiners used to construct chairs, as they did chests, before the seventeenth century. It is thought that that is how chairs started out—as chests with backs and arms added—and that is just what they looked like. The seat was boxlike, with no separate legs; the back and the arms were solid, perhaps to protect the sitter from drafts. Decoration was minimal—simply some Gothic tracery or linen-fold carving. Chairs were seats of honor, reserved at first for royalty, later for the master of the household and his wife. The common man sat on benches, stools, or chests. The stool had stretchers very near the floor for the feet so that they would not have to rest on the soiled rushes on the floor.

Sometimes the chairs had cloths thrown over them for decoration or warmth; sometimes cushions were used to soften the hard seat. This is where needlework enters the picture. The cushions for these chairs were made of rich fabrics befitting the sitter. They were often embroidered in canvas work or needlepoint with couched metal threads. The designs were generally floral, simply shaded, and rather symmetrical. One or two motifs were repeated in a set pattern with a border around the edge. The cushion was then trimmed with deep and profuse fringe.

Around the middle of the sixteenth century, curule or X-frame chairs were revived in England from ancient times. Cloth was stretched from side to side to form the seat and from one upright to the other to form the back; sometimes the whole frame was covered with cloth. The

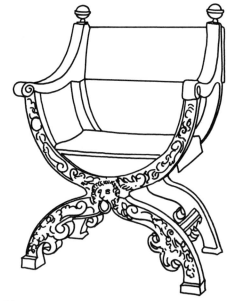

X-style walnut chair, mid-sixteenth century.

user's arms might be embroidered on the back panel. In France about the same time caquetoire chairs were being made. These chairs had real legs, instead of being boxes with backs, and were wider in the front than in the back. The backs were thus rather narrow and were often highly carved. The arms curved downward and were slightly rounded.

During the sixteenth century the need for fortified barracks-like houses lessened, and smaller and more comfortable homes were built. From 1553 to 1603 England was ruled by women, and the feminine touch was shown in a greater interest in the arts and more courtly manners. (It must be said, though, that Henry VIII encouraged craftsmen from Holland, France, and Italy to settle in England.) A rich merchant class arose and the finer things were no longer restricted to royalty. Furniture, jewelry, and clothing became much more elaborate. The English adapted the style of the caquetoire to their needs, giving it a wide, highly carved, and sometimes inlaid back and a wider seat both front and back. Cushions were now a real necessity for the hard wooden chairs. The tent stitch, known today as the half cross-stitch, was used so much for cushions that this type of embroidery was known as

cushion work. The embroidery and materials became much more
sumptuous. Silks and metal threads, velvet, and cloth of silver were
used for cushions. The designs were much more naturalistic than before,
with considerably more detail and shading. The floral designs were
usually intertwined symmetrically in knots and frets. The Tudor rose,
pomegranates, and other fruits were favorite themes.

Panoramic scenes with elaborate borders were used for long cushions and for bed furnishings. The scenes, often pastoral in content,
showed families sitting about; houses were in correct perspective, but
the trees boasted enormous fruit; tiny animals gamboled; and very large
worms and butterflies filled in empty spaces. Mythology and the Bible
were sources of inspiration. The people in these tent-stitch scenes were
sometimes clothed in costumes contemporaneous with the story and

Late sixteenth-century
cushion cover,
English. Cross-stitch
and long-arm cross-
stitch in silk and wool.
Victoria and Albert
Museum. Crown
Copyright.

sometimes with the embroiderer. The more intricate of these canvases closely resembled the tapestry of the time and were beautifully designed and executed.

Other sources of design in this period and in the seventeenth century were bestiaries and herbals. Pattern books just for the embroiderer were published on the Continent in the last quarter of the sixteenth century. One of the best known was Jacques Lemoine de Morgue's *Le Clef des Champs,* published in France in 1586. The designs were applied to the linen canvas with black ink and then embroidered in color to the taste of the embroiderer. Shading was indicated by a light gray wash. An interesting footnote to the sixteenth-century canvas work in England is that the landscape canvases did not have the excessive number of hillocks and hummocks that they acquired in the next cen-

Late sixteenth-century cushion cover depicting the judgment of Solomon, French. Victoria and Albert Museum. Crown Copyright.

Borders, English, ca. 1600, silk and wool on linen. Victoria and Albert Museum. Crown Copyright.

tury. The importation in the seventeenth century of East Indian palampores with their tree-of-life motif introduced the predilection for handling landscape in this way. It became a staple of Jacobean crewel embroidery design.

Crests were another popular design motif. The crest was laid on a field of flowers and surrounded with an ornate border. The linen used as canvas in Elizabethan times was quite fine, permitting the embroiderers to use a great deal of detail in their designs. A favorite variety of decoration for cushions was appliquéd slips. These were single figures of flowers or animals copied from herbals and bestiaries, worked in crewels or silk in tent stitch, then cut out and applied to silk, velvet, or satin. The edges were outlined with couched gilt threads. Fancy gilt fringe and lace trimmed the edges of such cushions. Interlocking Gobelin stitch, cross-stitch, Queen (or rococo) stitch, and, of course, tent stitch were used on these slips.

Toward the end of the sixteenth century, chairs assumed a more austere and architectural form; carving became simpler and was used less as upholstery was used more. The backs of chairs were upholstered as well as the seats, and both were heavily trimmed with braid and

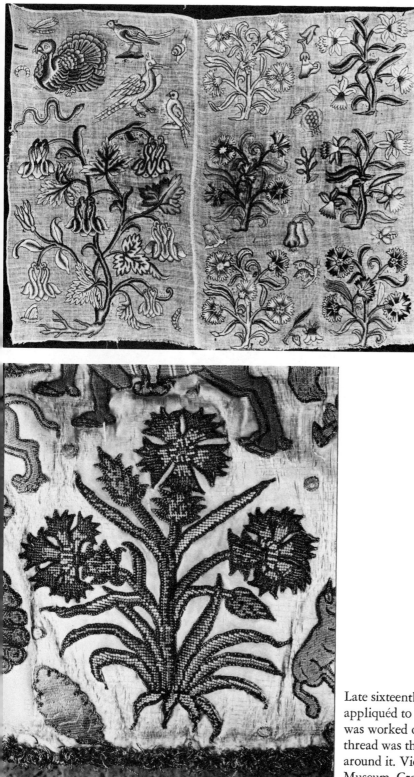

A panel of slips preserved
unused. English, early seventeenth
century. Victoria and Albert
Museum. Crown Copyright.

Late sixteenth-century slip
appliquéd to silk. The daffodil
was worked on linen; silver gilt
thread was then couched
around it. Victoria and Albert
Museum. Crown Copyright.

fringe. In France, Henry IV had established a silk factory where velvets, brocades, and brocatelles were woven. Velours d'Utrecht, a woolen velvet, was used in both France and Holland. Authorities disagree as to whether the French version of this material was called moquette or whether moquette was something else. In France the material used many colors and small designs; the Dutch preferred more figurative designs such as houses, animals, and hunting scenes.

Cushion cover of black silk velvet. Silver gilt and silver thread were used. English, late sixteenth or early seventeenth century. Victoria and Albert Museum. Crown Copyright.

CHAPTER THREE

1603-1643

The arbitrary dates of 1603 to 1643 cover the beginning of the reign of James I of England and Scotland to the end of the reign of Louis XIII. Foreign trade among the countries of Europe increased exposure to different styles and arts. Merchants purchased for themselves and their customers things seen before only in royal palaces. Kings took a greater interest in building and decorating their royal houses. In England the ideas of Jan V. de Vries, the Flemish architect, sculptor, and designer of furniture and ornament, influenced the court of James I. Later Inigo Jones, England's first royal architect, was graced with royal patronage and perhaps inspired the rising interest in Palladian architecture. Flemish, German, and Huguenot craftsmen were encouraged to settle in England.

In France, Flemish and Spanish influence was strong in the decorative arts. During the reign of Charles I the French and English royal houses were related by marriage and the trading of ideas and fashions increased.

During this period needlework was used for upholstery in both France and England. The English continued to use slips on satin and velvet. The cross-stitch was used more than before. Near the end of her reign Elizabeth I chartered the East India Company to begin trade with India. So began the importation of the painted and printed cottons so dear to the heart of the crewel embroideress, the East Indian palampores. The designs were a blend of Indian tradition, Chinese patterns,

35

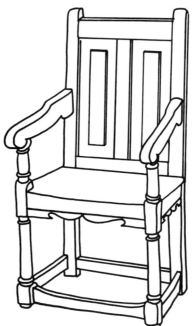

Connecticut wainscot chair,
mid-seventeenth century.

and English ideas of what Indian chintzes should look like. By the end
of the reign of Charles I this trade was well established and so was the
Jacobean style of crewel embroidery. At first the chintzes showed exotic
sprigs of flowers printed closely together with a few very small tree-
like forms in the borders. During the reign of Charles I the famous
tree-of-life design evolved with bold stems surrounding flowers of
diverse varieties, all on the same tree. The leaves were worked in outline
and then filled with abstract patterns having little to do with nature.
The colors were limited; monochromatic greens were not unusual.

Leather, both plain and tooled, was used as upholstery. It was
nailed to the frame of the chair with large mushroom-headed tacks. In
France, moquette, velvet, and damask were used, and the backs and
seats of the chairs were still heavily fringed. In America the colonists
depended on imported fabric or the woolen fabric they could manufacture themselves. In 1638 in Ipswich, Massachusetts, a fulling mill
was established where twenty workers were employed in the process of
scouring and pressing broadcloth.

English	French
Strapwork with arabesques	Strapwork
Grotesques	Cartouches
Moorish geometric patterns	Oval shields
Animals and flowers, realistic and fantastic	Fat cherubs
	Masks
Guilloches	Grotesques
Fruits	Swags of fruit and flowers
East Indian tree of life	Geometric stars and diamond shapes
Hunting scenes	Hunting scenes
Scenes from the classics	Religious themes
	Scenes from the classics

Damask pattern, Italian, mid-seventeenth century.

CHAPTER FOUR

1643-1703

This period was dominated by the Sun King, Louis XIV, who ascended the throne of France in 1643. England at this time was undergoing the turmoil of the overthrow of Charles I, the Commonwealth, and then the Restoration period under Charles II, later James II, and finally a peaceful period under William and Mary.

The best words to describe the furniture and decoration in the time of Louis XIV would be elegant, baroque, symmetrical, and stately. Here was a king who reveled in beauty and made it the business of the state to encourage the arts. He was aided in this by his economic adviser, Jean Baptiste Colbert, who was interested in textiles. With the advice of Colbert, the king in 1662 purchased the Gobelins, then a family-owned tapestry factory, and made it the royal manufactory of court furniture. Tapestry, furnishings, silver, and textiles were turned out, much of them for use in Louis's pet project, the decoration of Versailles. Another tapestry factory, Beauvais, was state-directed but privately owned.

The King chose able men to organize and direct these projects. Charles Le Brun, a painter, was named the king's art director. His influence was felt in all aspects of the arts, from furniture to tableaux for the king's amusement (in which Louis usually took part). Daniel Marot was another brilliant designer in Louis's court. His talents covered architectural details, furniture, and textiles. He fled France when Louis XIV revoked the Edict of Nantes in 1685. After a stay in Holland, where he came under the patronage of William of Orange, he followed his patron

Flemish seventeenth-century needlepoint chair. The needlework may be of a later date. Courtesy of the Virginia Museum, Gift of Mrs. Hildreth Scott Davis in memory of her late husband, George Cole Scott.

to England. Other Huguenot craftsmen fled France at the same time, thus spreading French ideas and taste into Holland, England, and even America. Other designers who were favorites of the king were Jean Bérain, noted for his tapestry designs, and André Charles Boulle, known for his tortoiseshell- and brass-inlaid furniture.

Walnut, in use since the reign of Louis XIII, was still a favorite wood, but fruitwood, box, and ebony were also used. Furniture was gilded, lacquered, and trimmed with ormolu mountings. Toward the end of Louis XIV's reign, embroidered silks as well as chintzes and muslins were imported from the Orient. Satins, velvets, patterned taffetas, damasks, and gold and silver brocades were used for upholstery. Tapestry was used extensively as upholstery at the end of Louis's reign. The designs were quite elaborate, often depicting a vase of flowers set in a frame of scrolled curves. The design on the back of chairs did not always match the seat design. It might show instead a design of scattered flowers. The Beauvais tapestry factory wove tapestry to be used especially for upholstery. Fringe was still used at the bottom of the backs of the chairs and around the lower edge of the seats. Gold and silver lace was appliquéd on velvet in arabesque designs on the tall backs of the chairs, with an elegant effect.

Tent stitch and Point de Hongrie in a flame pattern were used often for upholstery. A distinction should be made here between Florentine stitch and Point de Hongrie. Florentine stitch is an upright stitch over a consistent number of threads or mesh row after row. Point de Hongrie is an upright stitch too, but the number of mesh over which it is worked may vary from row to row—for instance, two mesh for one row and then four mesh for the next. Furthermore, sometimes the length of the stitch varies from four to two mesh in the same row,

Armchair, English, ca. 1685, from Drayton House, Northamptonshire. Victoria and Albert Museum. Crown Copyright.

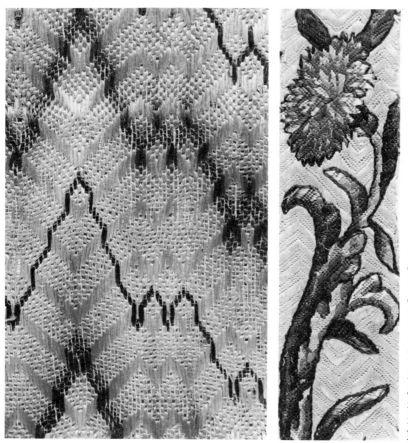

FAR LEFT: An example of Point de Hongrie, silk on canvas. Photo: Philip L. Coltrain.

LEFT: An example of Point de Hongrie. The pattern of the stitches goes in four directions in the head of the flower. Photo: Philip L. Coltrain.

resulting in a very complicated pattern. Both forms of bargello, as we call it today, may be worked in a flame pattern. Florentine stitch and Point de Hongrie were not the only stitches used to produce a flame pattern. Historic Deerfield, Inc., has a beautiful William and Mary wing chair worked in the kalem or knit stitch, which was often used in the eighteenth century for the flame pattern. Another stitch used for the flame pattern is called the Irish stitch. It is worked over four mesh for each stitch, but it rises two mesh each time, making a four-two step, to use technical language.

European needleworkers in the seventeenth century favored large flame patterns in Florentine stitch or Point de Hongrie. Flame-like en-

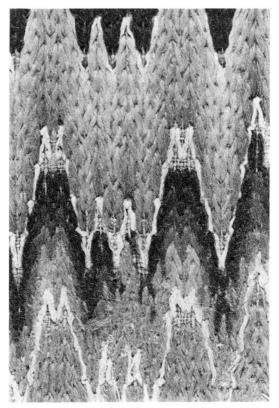

An example of the kalem or knit stitch in
a flame pattern. Photo: Philip L. Coltrain.

closed shapes, some of them quite complex, but all fairly large, were the
style in the early eighteenth century. As the century wore on, patterns
became smaller and considerably more complex and enclosed. Point de
Hongrie was used less and less, and the Irish stitch and the brick stitch
were favored. By the end of the eighteenth century the patterns were
just an inch or two in height as compared with four or five inches at
the beginning of the century. In America the colonists went their merry
way doing flame patterns throughout the century. Diamond-shaped patterns and carnation patterns also graced many a chair seat and pocket-
book in America.

But to return to our original subject, Philibert Balland directed
the embroidery workshop at Gobelins; there was another such workshop at Saint-Cyr. It is said that Versailles had embroideries with chased

Louis XIV chair, late seventeenth century.

silver plaques for the human parts. Perhaps this is the source of the Moravian embroideries, popular in America in the late eighteenth and early nineteenth centuries, in which painted silk was used for the faces of the people.

The classic chair leg for the Louis XIV style is a square vase-like shape that joins directly into the seat of the chair or into a molded frame. It has a square ankle and a splayed-out square foot. The four legs are joined by curved stretchers. Toward the end of the period, an early cabriole leg appeared, also joined by curved stretchers. A slightly coiled foot led to a slim ankle, up to a slightly flexed knee that joined the seat with a flourish of carving. These chairs were called fauteuils. They had what we call today a slip seat, that is, a wooden frame that was covered with padding and upholstery material and could be removed from the frame of the chair, so that the upholstery could be changed with the seasons. Light fabrics were used in the spring and summer, and rich ones in the fall and winter. Many colors were used during the long reign of Louis XIV, but red was the favorite. Settees or canapés appeared at this time, usually made to go en suite with the chairs. Large seat cushions were used on the canapés.

Turkey-work side chair, Dutch or
English, ca. 1650, oak frame.
Courtesy of the Brooklyn
Museum, Gift of Frank L. Babbott.

Styles in England before the Commonwealth were a little more austere. Chair legs were columnar, joined with a stretcher near the floor. Chair backs were low but upholstered, as were the seats. Needlework was a common upholstery fabric, as well as velvet. The needlework designs were mainly floral, sometimes including a family crest on the back. Cross-stitch was a favorite, though tent stitch was used on finer material. Turkey work was also used. Most authorities feel that turkey work was woven, not stitched, that is, that a row of Ghiordes knots were tied and then a weft thread woven over them to be followed by another row of knots. There is a possibility that it was stitched on a ready-made canvas. The background of some existing examples has rotted away (probably because of the dye used for the dark background), so it is difficult to tell whether it was woven or stitched. One wonders if turkey work were made in imitation of more costly imported cut velvets.

Jacobean chair, ca. 1660.   Jacobean stool, ca. 1660.

During the time of Oliver Cromwell, chair styles stayed the same except that the common upholstery material was leather, secured with brass nail heads. The restoration of the monarchy brought more opulent styles back to England. The legs of the square chair popular during the Commonwealth acquired spiral turnings. This square chair was known as a farthingale chair because it accommodated the wide, full skirts in style in the seventeenth century. Settees were made in much the same style, but with higher backs. The daybed came into style at this time. A long, loose cushion was laid on it, sometimes upholstered in Florentine stitch in a flame pattern.

Christopher Wren, the architect, brought French and Palladian influences to English style. Houses became less somber; the walls were wood-paneled as before, but the ceilings were plastered and colorfully painted instead of timbered. Sash windows, used after 1670, opened up rooms to more light. The great carver Grinling Gibbons decorated paneling with carvings of festoons of fruit, flowers, and foliage. Furniture styles were greatly influenced by the Dutch. Chair backs were heightened; legs acquired S curves, C curves, and Flemish scrolls. The backs

Walnut armchair, English, ca. 1670. Courtesy of the Virginia Museum, Gift of Mrs. Edwin Darius Graves, Jr., 1952.

Jacobean armchair, ca. 1685.

of the chairs became more open with carving, and caning was set in the high backs and seats of the chairs. Painting and gilding became stylish as the chairs became more intricately carved and turned.

Silk velvets in bright colors, as well as plain and tooled leather, were favorite seat coverings. Brocaded silks from Genoa and Genoese damask were used, the Italian silks sometimes brocaded in silver and gold. China silks with asymmetrical patterns and Chinese embroideries were popular. Silks were imported from France and India, but some were woven in England by the Huguenots. Turkey work was still in vogue.

This was a great period for needlework in England. Gros point, petit point, cross-stitch, and Queen (rococo) stitch were still used in needlepoint. Sometimes crewel stitches were worked on the same piece of embroidery—satin stitch, long and short, couched threads, and French knots. The crewel stitches preferred then were chain stitch, stem stitch, long and short, satin stitch, and different kinds of buttonhole stitch. The stems on crewel embroideries worked at the time of the Restoration became somewhat thinner. The trees of life sprouted from well-defined hummocks or little clusters of hills. Animals and very large fanciful birds were introduced into the designs.

Fringes were heavy and often decorated further with tassels attached to the fringe. Settees looked like joined chair backs; toward the end of the century they sprouted wings, out-scrolled arms, and up-

Side chair, English, ca. 1690.

holstery. Two large cushions softened the seats. Complicated floral designs surrounding panels of landscapes or allegorical scenes were worked in tent stitch for the settees.

When William of Orange ascended the throne of England in 1689, style took a definite turn to the Baroque. Daniel Marot, the Huguenot refugee, followed his patron to England where he continued to use French motifs and ideas. Gerrit Jensen, of Flemish and Dutch extraction, was famous for his marquetry and lacquer work, following the style of the Frenchman Boulle in his work with metal and tortoiseshell.

Chairs of the William and Mary period had high backs with a center portion that came down almost to the seat. Vase-like legs were joined by curving stretchers just above round ball-like feet. Very late in the seventeenth century a slight cabriole leg was introduced. It is said that the cabriole leg came originally from China. In France, as men-

William and Mary wing chair, probably English, late seventeenth century. The wood has been painted black and the carving touched with gilt. The flame pattern was worked in kalem or knit stitch. Courtesy of the Shelburne Museum, Shelburne, Vermont.

tioned before, the foot had a slight whirl. In England it was in the shape of a hoof and sometimes a little slippered foot. The ball-and-claw foot appeared around 1700. The edges of the seats were nearly always trimmed with fringe. Stools were very popular. They were usually rectangular in shape with an ornate X stretcher, and the seat was ringed profusely.

Slipcases reached England during William and Mary's reign. Genoese velvets in mixed colors were used for upholstery, crimson and green being the preferred colors. Other fabrics were brocatelles, damasks, and brocades. Crewel was fashionable as upholstery. It is known that Queen Mary herself embroidered crewel coverings for chairs and a stool. Cross-stitch and Florentine stitch in a flame pattern were stylish too, the latter particularly so for corner chair seats. This style of chair continued in popularity right through the eighteenth century.

Wing chair, English, ca. 1690. The needlework shows Saul anointing David. Courtesy of the Metropolitan Museum of Art, Collection of Irwin Untermeyer, 1964.

William and Mary banister-back chair,
American, ca. 1700.

Chair styles in the Colonies were very much like the English styles, allowing a few years for their transposition overseas. Inventories such as one done of the worldly goods of Captain Kidd's wife in 1692 in New York mention a dozen turkey-work chairs. Mention of turkey-work chairs is also made in early inventories of important men such as governors. Also mentioned are velvet and satin cushions, and even silver lace trim. A more common type of chair was the slat-backed turned chair with a rush seat made from local woods by local craftsmen. If the seat was softened at all, it was with a chair pad tied to the back. Chair pads used on more ornate William and Mary–style chairs should be attached with cords and deep tassels. The pads should be knife-edged rather than boxed.

Though linen and hemp were grown in the South as early as 1659 and the Huguenots were producing some silk, the colonists used woolen fabrics for the most part for their upholstery. This was especially true after the Wool Act of 1699, which forbade the colonists to export wool back to England. Thereafter three-quarters of the wool in the Colonies was domestic. The fabrics used had names like camlet, wool with some silk or goat's hair; kersey, a light twilled wool; perpetuana, a smooth worsted with more warp than weft threads, sometimes made of mohair; and linsey-woolsey, woven with a linen warp and a woolen weft. Serge and broadcloth were also used.

MOTIFS

English	French
Dolphins	Scallop shells
Acanthus leaves	Acanthus leaves
Cherub heads	Diamond shapes
Birds, especially eagles	Chinese dragons, pagodas
Flowers in scrolls, C scrolls, and S scrolls	Fauns and satyrs
	Masks
Grapes	Caryatids
Seed pods	Roman helmets
Swags of fruit, flowers	Laurel, olive, and palm leaves
Chinoiserie	Grotesques, animal and human
Cartouches	Religious symbols
Italian grotesques	Rare animals
Strapwork	Musical instruments
Pastoral scenes	Vases of flowers
Classical scenes, often including James II	Mythological themes glorifying Louis XIV, Louis as Apollo, Maria Theresa as Diana
Very detailed garlands	
Fish	
Shells	Symmetry
C scrolls embellished with foliage	Quivers and arrows
	Stars with rays around them
Butterflies	Architectural columns and entablature as frame
Masks	
Caryatids	Flame stitch
Vegetables	
Architectural columns entwined with fantastic flowers	
Flame stitch	

CHAPTER FIVE

1703-1727

The years 1703 through 1727 cover the reign of Queen Anne and King George I in England and the end of the reign of King Louis XIV, the Régence, and the beginning of the reign of Louis XV in France. Though the historical dates are rigid, the change in furniture styles was more gradual. Let it be said that the magnificence of the Sun King's court gently eased away from pageantry and pomp to a more relaxed and romantic way of life. The Régence provides a link between the two reigns in more than just government. The fauteuil became even more comfortable-looking during the Régence, retaining a stretcher between the legs but becoming lower and larger in the seat. During Louis XV's reign the stretcher disappeared, the seat became even lower and more cushioned, and the back more comfortable and larger. The court seemed relieved to turn away from the formality of Louis XIV to the gaiety of the court of Louis XV.

Claude Gillot and his pupil Antoine Watteau set the tone for this period. Think of Watteau's paintings and you can sense the feeling of lightheartedness and frivolity in his use of warm, glowing, almost sensuous colors. During the Régence the beginning of the rocaille style began to take form. *Rocaille* means "rock grottoes," but in ornament it translates to the use of fantastic natural forms, many curves, and asymmetry. Gillot and Watteau were both excellent designers of rocaille or rococo ornament. Their particular forte was elaborate and imaginative designs using themes from the Italian Comedy, singeries, and Turkish

Régence fauteuil.

scenes. The singeries showed monkeys in fanciful occupations such as playing musical instruments, sometimes dressed in costumes. Romantic scenes set in frames of trees and architectural forms depicted couples ice skating, swinging in swings, or playing games.

Tapestry was still very popular for upholstery, as was needlework of all kinds. Needlepoint and tapestry were designed especially for the chairs on which they were used. The borders of the designs followed the frame of the back of the chair, the shape of the seat, and the arm pads. Fanciful arabesque structures contained the design, decorated with masks of satyrs, animals, and the scallop shell. Scattered floral pieces were worked too, the flowers resembling huge peonies with a ribbon bow tucked into the pattern. What little background showed was of a light color.

The actual reign of Queen Anne covered only twelve years, but the furniture period that bears her name covers a style and trend that continued for two or three times that number of years. Form and proportion best describe the Queen Anne period. To most people Queen Anne is a classic, easily identifiable style. It is a nearly perfect balance of richness and simplicity. Later styles may be bolder or more elegant,

American Queen Anne side chair. The bargello seat is original to the chair. From a private collection; the owner has two of the chairs. White outlines the diamond shapes on one seat and black is used on the other; otherwise, the colors—blue, red, gold, and green—do not differ. Photo: Beatley and Gravitt, Richmond, Virginia; copied from a Helga Studio photo.

Slip seat of the American Queen Anne side chair. Photo: Beatley and Gravitt, Richmond, Virginia; copied from a Helga Studio photo.

but Queen Anne retains a purity of line and proportion that pleases the eye even today. The charm of a Queen Anne chair probably lies in the repetition of the cyma curve. There is a slight cyma curve in the splat of the back, another in the cabriole leg, and sometimes the splat echoes the curve in its outline. A shell ornament often decorates the back or the front apron of the seat; acanthus leaves might curl over the knees of the cabriole legs. The back legs are usually not cabriole but flare gently back. The arms of armchairs are curved easily outward, repeating the rounded-off corners on the back of the chair. The seat of the chair might be rounded too, in what is called a balloon seat—not really round but shaped more like a scallop shell.

For the most part, side chairs made during Queen Anne's brief reign did not have upholstered backs. Those that did were framed in a simple carved border or were shortened and rounded and had no fram-

Queen Anne side chair with crewel seat. The pattern fits the chair so well, one could presume that the seat was made especially for the chair. Courtesy of the Metropolitan Museum of Art, Gift of Mrs. J. Insley Blair, 1946.

Side chair (one of a set of eight), Queen Anne style, English, ca. 1710. Note the man at bottom right pumping steam for the calliope. Courtesy of the Brooklyn Museum, Gift of Mrs. H. A. Metzger.

Detail from the back of one of the Queen Anne side chairs from the Metzger Gift. The foliage, birds, and hunters are worked in petit point; the rest of the work is gros point. The chairs are made of walnut and birch, ca. 1710. Courtesy of the Brooklyn Museum, Gift of Mrs. H. A. Metzger.

ing at all. During the time of George I, Queen Anne style went through a more decorated phase, about which more will be said later.

Queen Anne style lends itself nicely to the wing or easy chair. The crest of the back was slightly rounded; the wings had a flat leading edge that flowed into the level of the arm and then into outscrolling that in turn flowed down to the leg. The seat had a loose cushion. The profile view of a Queen Anne wing chair shows a flat line from the top of the wing down to the bottom of the upholstered part. This is also true of Georgian chairs. Later wing styles show in profile that the wing goes down to the arm and that the arm then extends onto the back of the

Chair back, English, early eighteenth
century. Parts of the flowers are
worked in petit point. Victoria and
Albert Museum. Crown Copyright.

Queen Anne side chair, American,
ca. 1730. Courtesy of Yale Univer-
sity Art Gallery, the Mabel Brady
Garvan Collection.

chair. Thus it looks as if the wing were resting on the arm of the chair.
On wing chairs of both Queen Anne and Georgian styles, it was cus-
tomary to cover or pipe the seams of the upholstery with braid of a contrasting color.

Queen Anne upholstered settees have a slightly high straight back
with cabriole legs; they often have a long, loose cushion. Needlepoint,
usually of a scattered floral design, was a typical covering. The scattered
flowers were of rather large proportions resembling chrysanthemums or
peonies with appropriate foliage. Wing chair designs used the scattered
flowers motif, the tree-of-life pattern, and sometimes pastoral scenes

Queen Anne wing chair,
American, New England,
ca. 1725. Courtesy of the
Metropolitan Museum of Art,
Gift of Mrs. J.
Insley Blair, 1950.

on the back. The pastoral scene might spread over onto the wings of the chair, the whole design set into a simple curving frame. Green and brown, as well as medium and dark blue, were used as background colors.

Crewel and silk embroidery were used for later solid-backed side chairs. Crewel was used for slip seats, but as mentioned before it is difficult to determine whether it was original to the chair or a cut-down bed curtain. However, there is one kind of crewel seat that seems to be especially made for that purpose; that is the allover pastoral design worked on closely woven linen in a flat long stitch. A combination of the long and short stitch and the encroaching Gobelin stitch would be the best way to describe it. Usually worked in horizontal rows, it permits gradual shading. Other stitches such as the chain stitch, the stem stitch,

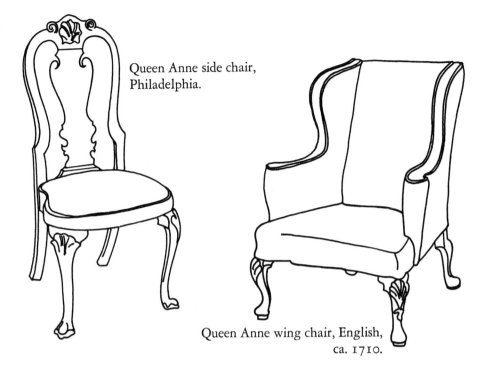

Queen Anne side chair, Philadelphia.

Queen Anne wing chair, English, ca. 1710.

and the satin stitch were used as accents. The flat stitch was used to cover the grounds completely, and it was also used just for the grass and trees on other more conventional pieces. On occasion it was combined with the tent stitch.

Very elegant slipcases were made of silk and then embroidered in silk with sprigs of flowers. Needlepoint slipcases were made for upholstered-back side chairs; they pulled down like a tightly fitting tea cozy. Because of the relative simplicity of the Queen Anne chair, the textiles used for seat covers tended to be plain. Silk or wool velvet and moreen (morine) were two such fabrics used. Moreen is a woolen fabric with a watered pattern applied to the surface by passing it between hot rollers. It was a well-known fabric in the Colonies too.

Windsor chairs, those hoop-and-spindle-backed wooden chairs, came originally from Buckinghamshire in England and were in use in the seventeenth century. They achieved a popularity in the early eighteenth century that continues to the present day. Practically any style of needle-

The back of a Queen Anne wing chair, English, early eighteenth century. Parts of the pattern are worked in petit point wherever it would seem that the worker felt more detail was needed. Victoria and Albert Museum. Crown Copyright.

Side view of Queen Anne wing chair. Victoria and Albert Museum. Crown Copyright.

View of seat of Queen Anne wing chair. Victoria and Albert Museum. Crown Copyright.

work from Queen Anne on is therefore appropriate to use for a chair pad. Martha Washington made twelve seat pads for Windsor chairs at Mount Vernon, using a scallop repeat design.

Although the Queen Anne style was a late arrival in the Colonies, it soon made up for lost time and became so firmly entrenched that different regions evolved distinctive variations of their own. So distinc-

Queen Anne wing chair, English, early eighteenth century. Note the scallop shells on the knee of the cabriole legs. Also note the deer escaping the hunters on the inside and outside surfaces of the arms. Wool and silk. Courtesy of the Indianapolis Museum of Art, Gift of the Decorative Art Society of the Indianapolis Museum of Art. Photo: Robert Wallace.

tive are these variations that experts can identify the region at a glance. The colonists painted Queen Anne furniture, lacquered it, and combined lingering touches of the William and Mary style with it, called Country Anne or Transitional Queen Anne.

A separate room just for dining was known in France by the middle of the seventeenth century, but the idea did not really catch on in England until well into the eighteenth century. The practice of using one large table did not become established until the last quarter of the eighteenth century. Before that one to four small tables were used. Other meals were taken elsewhere in the house; the dining room was used only for dinner. It is safe to assume, then, that dining-room chairs as a special kind of chair were not a common thing in the English household until sometime in the mid-eighteenth century. Before that, large sets of chairs would have been made to grace a large hall or a stateroom.

The French were quite particular about having everything match. Chair fabrics matched, of course, but the ornamentation on all the furniture in a room matched too. Individual cabinetmakers supported by

Queen Anne floral chair seat design, American.

Queen Anne armchair, American.

Windsor chair, American.

Queen Anne Transitional side chair,
New England, early eighteenth century.

Windsor chair with cross-stitch
cushion made by Martha
Washington, one of several
made over a period of thirty-six
years for Windsor chairs.
The shells are worked in red
worsted on a gold worsted
ground highlighted with
yellow silk floss. Courtesy of
the Mount Vernon Ladies'
Association. Photo:
Bonnie Boyle.

Crewel chair seat (detail),
American, made by
Mrs. John Barrett, born 1718.
Courtesy of the National
Gallery of Art,
Washington, D.C., Index of
American Design.

Queen Anne chair seat, ca.
1710. This amusing pastoral
scene has vivid red and yellow
flowers in the border; the
background is light blue.
Courtesy of Benjamin
Ginsburg, Antiquary, New
York. Photo: Helga Photo
Studio.

PLATE I. *The back of an early eighteenth-century settee, English. One wonders why the lion is oblivious to the dog and griffin altercation. Courtesy of Benjamin Ginsburg, Antiquary, New York. Photo: Helga Photo Studio.*

PLATE 2. *Queen Anne settee, English. The needlepoint is original to this very fine settee. Note the scallop shell carved on the knee of each leg and the closely set nails attaching the upholstery to the frame. Courtesy of Benjamin Ginsburg, Antiquary, New York. Photo: Helga Photo Studio.*

PLATE 3. *Crewel embroidery taken from a Queen Anne pole screen. This illustrates the tree-of-life design and the early eighteenth-century style of filling every space. The embroiderer had quite an imagination; not one flower is repeated. Probably American. Courtesy of Benjamin Ginsburg, Antiquary, New York. Photo: Helga Photo Studio.*

PLATE 4. *This early eighteenth-century cushion cover is English and was worked in wool and silk. Some of the flower petals were worked in alternating rows of half cross-stitch and continental stitch, creating a ribbed effect. Courtesy of the Antiques Warehouse, Richmond, Virginia. Photo: Philip L. Coltrain.*

PLATE 5. *Needlework screen, French, first quarter of the eighteenth century. Some of the design is worked in petit point. The panels capture the flavor of needlework design of the period. Courtesy of the Indianapolis Museum of Art, Gift of the Children of J. K. Lilly, Jr.*

PLATE 6. *This design was adapted from an early eighteenth-century chair seat. The colors used were matched as closely as possible to the original. Photo: Philip L. Coltrain.*

PLATE 7. *An adaptation of a mid-eighteenth-century bargello pattern; only the wave or flame colors are close to the original ones. The diamond shapes in the original were varied in color as if the embroiderer were using up scraps of wool left over from other projects. See page 82 for a detail of the original work. Photo: Philip L. Coltrain.*

PLATE 8. *Crewel chair seat, worked by Anne Bradstreet of New England.*
This is a photograph of a drawing of the original seat which is in the collection
of the Boston Museum of Fine Arts. Courtesy of the National Gallery of Art,
Washington, D.C., Index of American Design.

PLATE 9. *Chippendale wing chair with the original Irish stitch bargello upholstery. New England, mahogany and maple. Courtesy of the Museum of Fine Arts, Houston, the Bayou Bend Collection.*

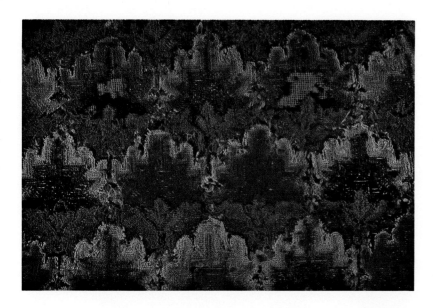

PLATE 10. *Original slip seat of country Chippendale side chair. See page 96. Courtesy of the Connecticut Historical Society, Hartford, Connecticut.*

PLATE 11. *Chippendale side chair with carnation bargello on the slip seat. See pages 23 and 80. The bargello pattern was worked in Irish stitch. Photo: Philip L. Coltrain.*

PLATE 13. *Crewel bouquet adapted from a Coromandel coast chintz of the last quarter of the eighteenth century. Crewel worked by Mrs. Grace Virginia Nelson with her choice of colors and stitches used in that period: stem stitch, chain stitch, satin stitch, French knots, and long and short stitch. Photo: Philip L. Coltrain.*

PLATE 12. *Brick stitch geometric design using original colors, mid-eighteenth century. See page 89 for graphed design and page 90 for the original work. Photo: Philip L. Coltrain.*

PLATE 14. *Classic Louis XVI bergère upholstered in tapestry. Note the drapery frame around the pastoral scene on the back of the chair. This chair, part of a set, was acquired from the collection of the late Myron Taylor. See page 102 for the canapé that is part of the same set. From the collection of the Honorable and Mrs. Marion Smoak. Photo: Bonnie Boyle.*

PLATE 15. *Seat of the Louis XVI balloon-mania chair shown on page 101. The balloon and the people are worked in half cross-stitch; the background is worked in Gobelin stitch. Courtesy of the Air and Space Museum of the Smithsonian Institution, Washington, D.C., Gift of Mr. and Mrs. William A. M. Burden.*

PLATE 16. *Design suitable for late eighteenth-
or early nineteenth-century chair; one might
call it a Hepplewhite-like stripe. See page 114
for graphed pattern. Photo: Philip L. Coltrain.*

PLATE 17. *Very early nineteenth-century
Berlin pattern designed by A. Philipson.*

PLATE 18. *Adaptation of a French Empire damask. The colors are the same but a single narrow stripe was left out, which was bracketed by two heavier stripes now shown as one. Photo: Philip L. Coltrain.*

PLATE 19. *Berlin pattern of neo-classical head and wreath of wheat husks, early nineteenth century.*

PLATE 20. *Basket of flowers,*
Berlin pattern designed by
A. Philipson, very early
nineteenth century.

PLATE 21. *Chair seat, New Jersey, ca. 1830, probably*
made for a fancy chair. Though it does not sit very
high off the ground fabric, the stitch used is a loopy one.
The stitch follows the curve of the design. Courtesy of
the Smithsonian Institution, Washington, D.C.

PLATE 22. *Empire stool with Berlin pattern tulip design, ca. 1810–1815. See page 133 for graphed design. Photo: Philip L. Coltrain.*

PLATE 23. *Griffins and lyre, early nineteenth-century neoclassical-style Berlin pattern designed by A. Philipson. See page 132 for graphed design.*

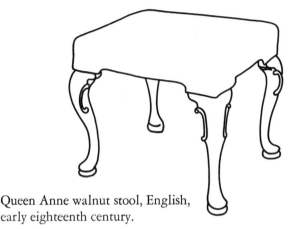

Queen Anne walnut stool, English,
early eighteenth century.

the state supplied furniture for the royal houses. The designs, as said
before, came from renowned artists and craftsmen. They were coordi-
nated by a special administration set up for that purpose. There was also
a strong guild system.

In England no such elaborate system existed. A monarch might
favor a particular designer, but the work was done under the direction
of the designer at the shops of craftsmen he chose to deal with or at his
own shop if he had one. There was no real coordination of design,
interior, and architecture until William Kent. He was the first true
interior decorator and designer, designing furniture to fit the architecture of rooms. He began working for royalty in 1721 when he came to
the attention of the Earl of Burlington. Kent favored the Palladian
school of architecture and introduced into a room such details as ornate
overmantels and pediments. Inigo Jones had used pediments in the previous century, but Kent used them on furniture and the rooms into
which the furniture went. Kent also favored the Venetian Baroque

Queen Anne wing chair. The needlepoint on this graceful chair is contemporaneous with the chair. The background is brown and the design is worked predominately in blue, green, and yellow. Courtesy of the Board of Regents of Gunston Hall Plantation, Lorton, Virginia. Photo: Bonnie Boyle.

style of furniture, highly ornamented and more massive than Queen Anne. He decorated many of the great houses in England during the reign of George I.

The cabriole leg was still in fashion, but it was much heavier, lower, and more highly carved. The wood used for Queen Anne was usually walnut and often walnut veneer; early Georgian furniture was made of mahogany. Whereas the scallop shell is associated with Queen Anne, the lion mask is associated with early Georgian and William Kent. It was sometimes carved on the knee of cabriole chair legs. Ball-and-claw feet, eagle-claw, and occasionally dragon-claw feet were appropriate for this style. Carved eagle heads terminated chair arms; dolphins were popular supports too. With the heavier leg the seat of the chair

Chair seat, English, second quarter of the eighteenth century, wool and silk, tent stitch and cross-stitch. Victoria and Albert Museum. Crown Copyright.

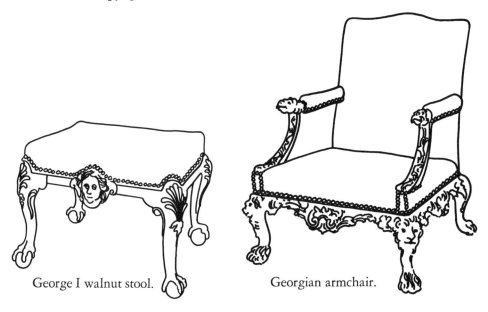

George I walnut stool.

Georgian armchair.

Needlepoint from the back of an early eighteenth-century settee. The design on the seat of this unusual piece matches the back. The colors are predominately blue, yellow, green, and white. Courtesy of Benjamin Ginsburg, Antiquary, New York. Photo: Helga Photo Studio.

was lowered and the back acquired a more serpentine curve. The English and French armchair styles were similar, the English being the more elaborate of the two.

Being more opulent in themselves, early Georgian chairs bore richer coverings. Cut velvets in rather florid damask patterns were used by Kent, as well as silk damasks. Crimson was a favored color.

The Queen Anne chairs still being made during this period absorbed some of the trend for ornamentation. Carved parts were gilded; more carving appeared on the knee and front apron of the seats. Lacquer was used over the entire chair.

Because of the time lag that occurred before a furniture style was adopted in the Colonies, it is difficult to be precise after 1770 as to the appropriateness of needlework to chair. The colonists did not always keep up with the current styles, particularly in the fields of bargello and crewel patterns. They went on using patterns that went out of style thirty years earlier in France and England, or they made up their own. If you wish to be precise, it is best to know the country of origin of the furniture for which you wish to embroider.

Bargello in Queen Anne's day was limited to three or four complementary colors for the more enclosed patterns. In the Colonies a greater range was allowed but the times had changed too. Pastoral scenes surrounded by flowers and foliage in bright, light colors in both tent stitch and cross-stitch were worked throughout the eighteenth century in the

Colonies and in England. The background color behind the foliage was often pastel. The classics and the Bible provided design ideas. In the Colonies even-weave linen was used for both crewel and canvas work, the former bleached and a finer count, the latter more open in weave and natural in color. The average canvas-work linen had a thread count of about twenty-four to the inch. Dimity, a material with a woven rib, was used for crewel too; it was much heavier than the dimity we know today.

Queen Anne commode stool from the master chamber at George Mason's home, Gunston Hall Plantation. The stool is walnut, made in Pennsylvania ca. 1745. The bed furnishings and slip seat on the stool in this bedroom are changed from damask in the winter to crewel in the summer. The stitches used include stem stitch, Roumanian stitch, and flat stitch. Courtesy of the Board of Regents of Gunston Hall Plantation, Lorton, Virginia. Photo: Bonnie Boyle.

Full view of crewel slip seat of Queen Anne commode stool, Gunston Hall Plantation. The flat stitch, a popular stitch in the eighteenth century, was worked in more than one way (see stitch diagrams at the end of the text). Without prying the stitches apart it is often difficult to tell which stitch was used on an old embroidery. Courtesy of the Board of Regents of Gunston Hall Plantation, Lorton, Virginia. Photo: Bonnie Boyle.

Crewel pattern adapted from eighteenth-century Indian chintz.

England	France
Queen Anne	Scallop shells
Scallop shells	Acanthus leaves
Acanthus leaves	Italian Comedy figures
Profuse foliage	Singeries
Pastoral scenes	Turkish scenes
Fantastic flowers placed against architectural arches	Pastoral scenes
	Scenes depicting the loves of Psyche
Chinoiserie	Chinoiserie
Allegorical scenes	Lozenges enclosing flowers in diaper patterns
Bouquets tied with ribbon	
George I	Bows and arrows
Lion masks	Garlands
Bellflower pendants	Espagnolettes (female busts topping thick cyma curves)
Putti sitting in shells	
Heavy swags of fruit	Rocaille
Greek fret friezes	Signs of the Zodiac
Bold eagle heads	Gods and goddesses such as Venus, Mercury, Apollo
Satyr masks	
Eggs and darts	Doves
Twisted dolphins	Bouquets in tall vases
Heavy arabesques	Arabesque frames
Double scallop shells	Musical instruments
Eight-point stars	Dolphins
Cherub heads with wings underneath	
Rosettes	
Laurel bound with ribbon	
Palmettes	
Beads and reels	

CHAPTER SIX

1727-1760

The Régence in France ended in 1723 and Louis XV ruled until 1774. George II ruled England from 1727 to 1760, which coincides nicely with the beginning of the neoclassical period in decoration and the age of Chippendale and Adam. If the previous period was characterized as being more relaxed and gay, this period would be said to be exuberant. Many consider the rocaille period to be the most graceful and elegant of all the French decorative periods.

Gilles-Marie Oppenord and Juste Aurèle Meissonier are considered to be the outstanding designers of the rocaille period, though neither lived past 1750. Oppenord was a holdover from the Régence, having been architect in chief to the regent. He and Meissonier are considered to be the leaders in establishing the rocaille style, Meissonier perhaps more than Oppenord. Meissonier was appointed by the king to be his official designer in 1725. His designs were incredibly ornate—some people felt to excess. Oppenord, on the other hand, felt that the architectural basis of a design should not be subordinated to the ornamentation. It was during this period that marquetry reached its height of craftsmanship in France. The men who did this work were called ébénistes. The ébéniste guild had very strict entrance requirements and limited its membership. Inspections were made by fellow craftsmen in the guild four times a year to maintain high standards. Jean François Oeben and Gilles Joubert are two of the best known of the ébénistes.

Of more concern to our study is Jean-Baptiste Oudry, who was

Two armchairs, upholstered in linen worked in crewels, American, ca. 1750. Courtesy of the Metropolitan Museum of Art, Bequest of Maria P. James, 1911.

the superintendent of the Beauvais tapestry factory and later of the Gobelins too. He designed a set of tapestries to illustrate "Les Fables de La Fontaine," "Les Comédiens de Molière," and "Les Métamorphoses." He also designed a series based on hunting and on motifs popular at the time, such as lovers' emblems. These small tapestries were just the size to be used on furniture, which proved to be a commercial success for the factory. Under Oudry tapestry became more like painting through the use of many more shadings of colors than had ever been used before. Unfortunately some of these shades were fugitive, and the delicacy of the effect is lost today. It was the style of these tapestries to place the humans on the back of the furniture and the animals on the seats.

François Boucher succeeded Oudry at the Gobelins late in the reign of Louis XV. He was court painter to the king as well. It was under Boucher that the frames surrounding tapestry scenes became oval.

Furniture of this period became lighter and smaller. Comfort was the keynote. Furniture was made for special-use rooms, such as a music room, and then decorated appropriately. Mahogany, cherry, and rosewood were used after 1740 because they were easy to carve. Roses were

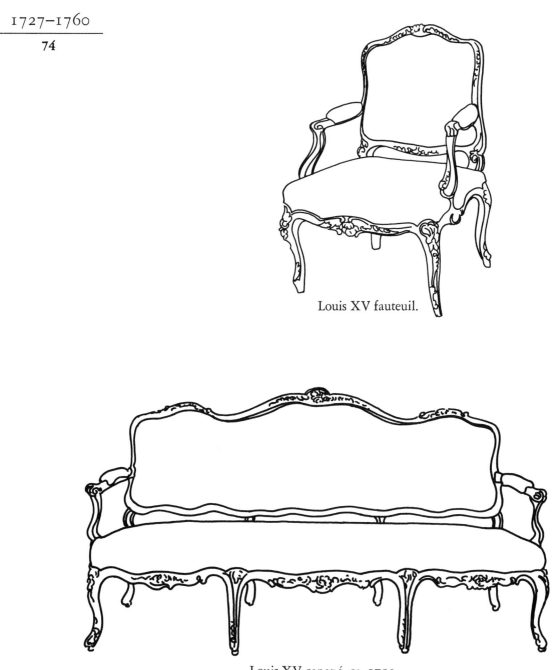

Louis XV fauteuil.

Louis XV canapé, ca. 1750.

Louis XV fauteuil, gilded, upholstered with Beauvais tapestry designed by Boucher. One of a suite of four chairs and one sofa. Courtesy of the Virginia Museum, Gift of Mrs. Ailsa Mellon Bruce.

a favorite carved motif. Caning was used on fauteuils and canapé seats, with cushions tied on for the winter months. Caning was also used for dining-room chairs. Tapestry, as mentioned before, was a very popular chair covering and needlepoint was equally so. Even the middle-class women had their needlepoint upholstery projects. In the summer chintz and linen, hand-painted in black outlines, were used for upholstery. Silk, especially painted in China for the French market with flowers and intertwining ribbons, was used. Taffeta, plain and striped satin, brocatelle, and plain and cut velvets were used for the winter months. Red morocco was used for dressing-table and writing-table chairs.

A new style of chair called a bergère evolved during this period. It was upholstered as one unit, with closed-in arms set back a bit from the front of the seat. A loose cushion was placed in the seat. It was the forerunner of several variations; one familiar to most people is the

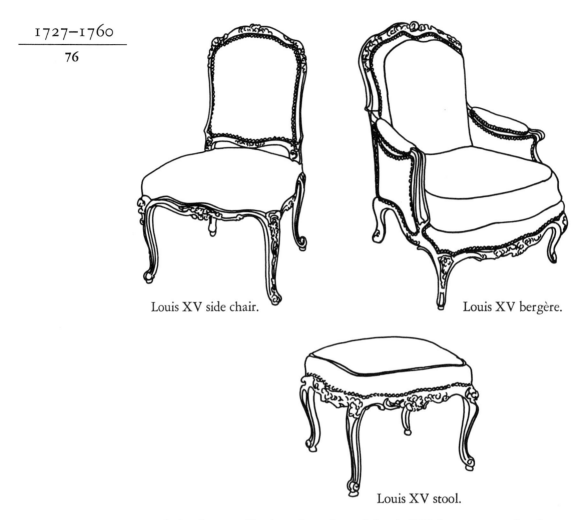

Louis XV side chair.

Louis XV bergère.

Louis XV stool.

chaise longue. During the reign of Louis XV it was a mark of great privilege and rank to be allowed to sit in the presence of the king, but the seat allowed was just a stool—elegant, upholstered, but nevertheless a stool. Stools are therefore an important part of the furniture of the period. This custom spread to England, where there were more stool designs after the middle of the eighteenth century.

It should be mentioned here that French provincial furniture usually denotes a plainer or country style of Louis XV or a simplified rococo style. Some lines from the period of Louis XVI are combined in later provincial furniture. There were distinctive differences in style

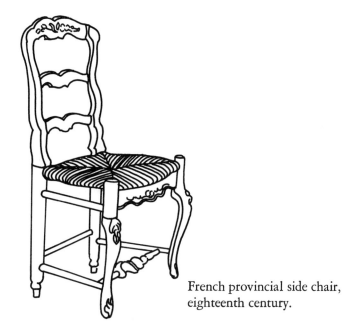

French provincial side chair,
eighteenth century.

from one province to another, just as in the American colonies there
were regional differences. Fruitwoods were used more than any other
wood. Needlepoint was very popular in the provinces. Simpler materials
such as painted or printed linen and cotton and mixes of silk and wool
were used as upholstery. Provincial chairs that were not upholstered
usually had cushion pads tied to the back and seat.

In England the classic Palladian style continued to be in fashion
until just past the middle of the century when Robert Adam and Thomas
Chippendale changed the English taste in favor of neoclassicism. The
French rocaille style was not entirely ignored, however. England had
its own rococo style. In France cast metal ornaments were attached to
case furniture and tables; the ornaments were called ormolu. What was
ormolu in France was carved and often gilded in England. Arm pads
appeared on wooden arms, and the backs of chairs acquired a serpentine
curve. Thomas Chippendale further developed English rococo in his
designs and publications, which will be taken up in the next chapter.

Though the word *sofa* had been coined earlier, this piece of furniture, an overstuffed, less formal version of a settee, gained acceptance
at this time.

Wing chair, English, mid-eighteenth century. Note the braid on the leading edge of the wings. Courtesy of the Virginia Museum.

Damasks, usually made of wool, and Genoese velvets were popular upholstery materials. The velvet was figured with lush plant forms in red or green with a light background.

Classical scenes continued to be a favorite design on wing chairs. Crowded Paisley-like flower designs surrounded the center design on the back. The scene was often worked in petit point with the rest of the work in cross-stitch. The materials used for canvas coarsened somewhat, making the designs a little less well defined. Russet and brown, and occasionally brighter shades of blue or even yellow, were used for what little background showed. Around 1730 in London, Robert Furber published a catalog that showed "The Twelve Months of Flowers"; in 1732 he produced a book, *The Flower Garden Displayed.* In the former, the flowers for each month were shown in huge bouquets thrust in

Walnut side chair, mid-eighteenth century, English. One of a set of six bequeathed by Lady W. S. Theobald. Victoria and Albert Museum. Crown Copyright.

Needlepoint chair covering, mid-eighteenth century, English. The design is in the style of Robert Furber's floral pictures shown in "The Twelve Months of Flowers." Courtesy of the Metropolitan Museum of Art, Collection of Irwin Untermeyer, 1974.

gray classical vases. These prints doubtless served as inspiration to many embroiderers, as many chair backs of the period testify. The background colors tended to be brighter with this type of design, a medium blue or gold not being unusual.

Shops in London sold kits for milady to work, with the pattern drawn on the canvas and the wools with which to work it included. In the Colonies there was seemingly enough of a market for pattern drawing that advertisements appeared in the *Boston Gazette* and the *Boston News-Letter* in the late 1730s for such services and for ready-made kits.

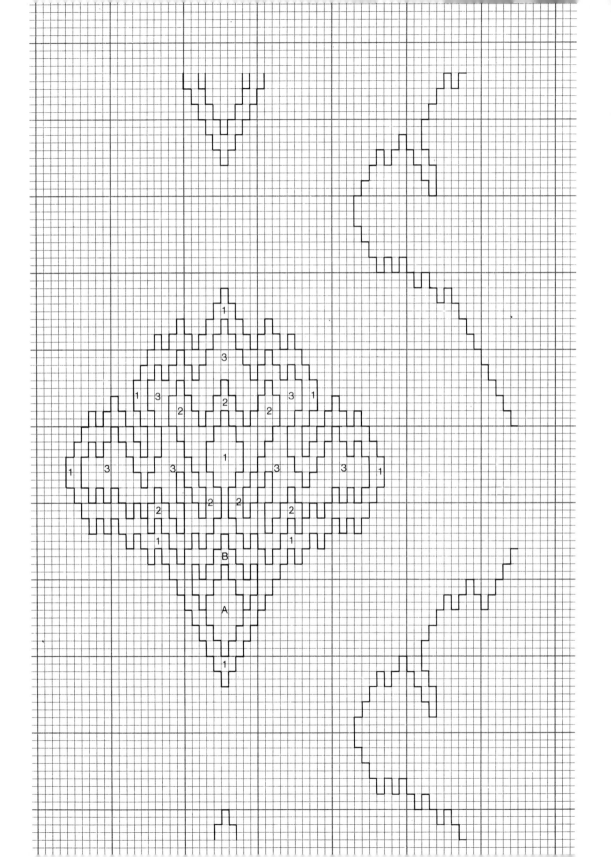

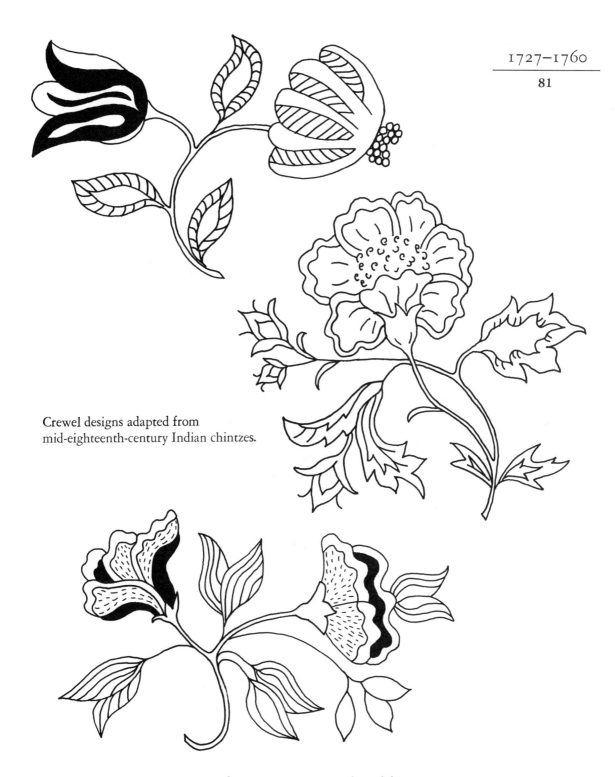

Crewel designs adapted from
mid-eighteenth-century Indian chintzes.

OPPOSITE: Bargello carnation pattern, mid-eighteenth century, adapted from an
example at the Victoria and Albert Museum, London.

The material for these kits was called canvas in these ads, but what was done on it was tent stitch rather than canvas work. Schoolmasters advertised the teaching of tent stitch, Irish stitch, and cross-stitch. Crewels, silks, and metal threads were advertised for sale to those who preferred to design their own work.

Special mention should be made of the "Fishing Lady" designs. It is believed that they were designed in or came from the shop of Mrs. Susannah Condy, who ran a shop and boarding school in Boston near the Old North Meeting House. She advertised that she had "patterns from London, but drawn by her much cheaper than English drawing. . . ." The Fishing Lady pattern was usually framed as a picture, but it is so much like the pastoral scene upholstery that it is worth mentioning. There was always a pretty lady sitting by a small body of water fishing. The picture included other people, sometimes working in the fields or just watching

Detail of a mid-eighteenth-century bargello pattern. The diamond shapes are about an inch and a half high. The waves or flames between the diamond shapes are shades of beige, the outline is brown, the diamond shapes are varied colors with no consistent pattern. See Plate 7 for a modern duplication of the pattern. Photo: Philip L. Coltrain.

OPPOSITE: Bargello pattern, adapted from mid-eighteenth-century example, probably English.

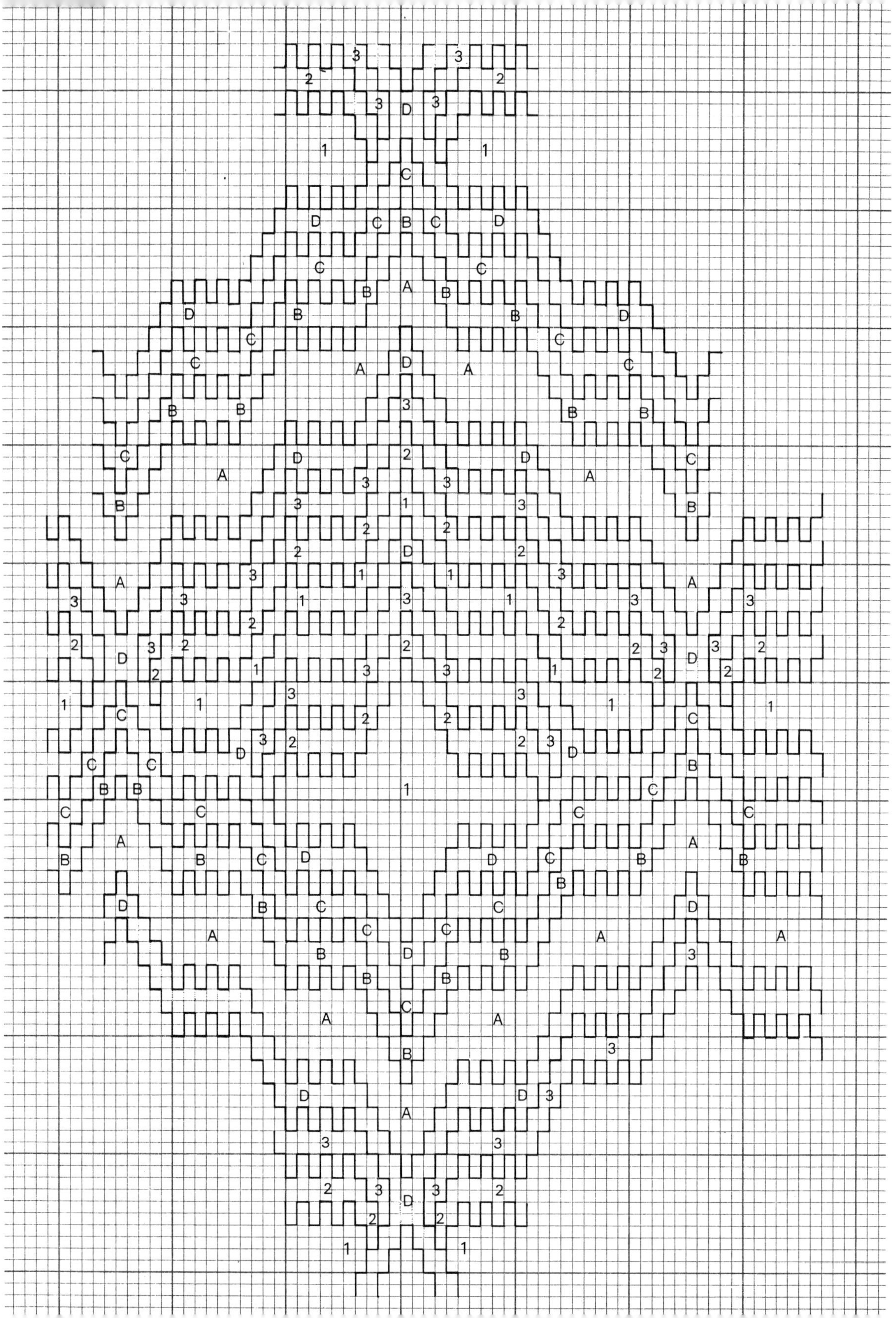

her or gathered around her for a little alfresco picnic. Birds, sheep, and dogs were shown, the dogs often up to some mischief.

In the Colonies the floral needlework in both crewel and needlepoint seems to be much more open than the English work of the same period. Perhaps it was because more of it was done by semiprofessional or amateur designers who are notoriously more shy about filling up space, or perhaps it was because the colonists preferred less opulent designs.

There is considerably more gradation in the background colors, no doubt because of the home dyeing of the wools used. English and French backgrounds are much more uniform. This is also true in bargello. One suspects that this was not by accident, that some bargello was worked just to use up scraps.

In Newport, Rhode Island, around 1730 to 1740, a very lovely Queen Anne slipper chair was covered with yellow glazed wool. White lace flower sprigs were then appliquéd here and there. Needless to say, this was not a common thing to do with lace, but it is worth mentioning if only to show that it is difficult to be dogmatic about just what is correct for a certain period or place.

As to the colors used in the Colonies, Alexander Fleming, dyer, in the *Boston Gazette* of May 14, 1754, stated that he could produce

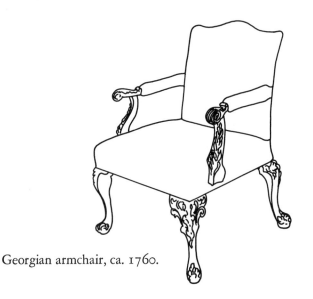

Georgian armchair, ca. 1760.

the following colors: "Scarletts, Crimsons, Pinks, Purples, Straws, Wine Colours, Sea-Greens, Saxon ditto, common Blues. . . ." He could dye linen yarn either "red blue green yellow or cloth colours . . . and all Colours on silks."

MOTIFS

England	France
Massed flowers in vases	Roses
Lion masks	Serrated and fringed acanthus
Human grotesques	leaves
Key and wave patterns	Bouquets in baskets
Eagle heads	Bouquets tied with ribbon
Bouquets tied with ribbon	Symbols of love and hunting
Acanthus leaves	tied with ribbon or crossed
Cabochons	Singeries
Architectural details	Romanticized chinoiserie
Rocaille arabesques	Musical instruments: flageolet,
Oriental or bizarre flower forms	violin, tambourine
Pastoral scenes	Wreaths of flowers
Biblical scenes	Commedia dell' arte characters:
Bargello	Pierrot, Scaramouche
	Arched branches, gnarled trees
	Nymphs
	Ram heads
	Cherubs
	Grapes
	Gadroons

CHAPTER SEVEN

1760-1795

Before neoclassicism took a firm foothold, England underwent its own rococo period. Chronologically we must go back a chapter. In 1754 Thomas Chippendale published the first edition of his pattern book *The Gentleman & Cabinet-Maker's Director*. (The third and final edition came out in 1762.) In it he showed designs derived from French rococo, the English version of chinoiserie, and Gothic. The Gothic vogue lasted just about ten years and was not as strong a fashion as were the other two. The Chinese trend was the rage of the early 1760s and was occasionally blended with rococo.

Chippendale was not the only cabinetmaker working at this time, but he is the best known and probably the most representative. The distinctive things about Chippendale's chair style are the serpentine back rail and the pierced back splat. The back of the chair was in the shape of either a cupid's bow or a reverse of that shape, with the center hump exaggerated. The latter style usually went with a cabriole leg, which Chippendale liked for his French-style chairs. The straight-legged chair was his preference for the dining room. Chippendale's plain straight leg is called a Marlborough leg. On it he sometimes added fretwork for his Chinese style or made it into a cluster of columns for Gothic styling. His favorite wood was mahogany, which he preferred for the dining room, the library, and the hall. He preferred gilded furniture for the drawing room. Carving was the main decoration on his furniture.

French chair from *The Gentleman & Cabinet-Maker's Director* by Thomas Chippendale, illustrating what he thought was an appropriate upholstery design for this style of chair. Photo: Philip L. Coltrain.

Armchair (one of a pair) in the French taste or style of Chippendale. English, ca. 1762. Courtesy of the Metropolitan Museum of Art, Collection of Irwin Untermeyer, 1964.

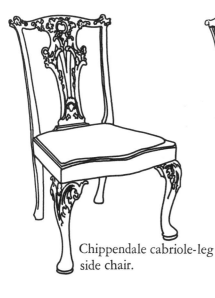

Chippendale cabriole-leg
side chair.

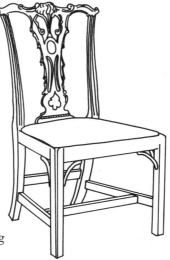

Chippendale side chair,
Marlborough leg, ca. 1755.

Pretzel ladder-back
side chair, Philadelphia.

Mahogany side chair, Chippendale,
Connecticut or Massachusetts, ca. 1765–
1785. Courtesy of the Museum of Fine
Arts, Houston, the Bayou Bend Collection.

Slip seat of the Bayou Bend Chippendale
chair—a particularly interesting
embroidery because it is designed in the
typical needlepoint style of flowers in
a vase but is worked in crewel embroidery
stitches. These include stem stitch, long
and short stitch, a form of flat stitch, and
chain stitch. Courtesy of the Museum
of Fine Arts, Houston, the Bayou Bend
Collection.

For upholstery Chippendale recommended tapestry, Spanish leather, damask, brocade, or needlework, to be secured with brass-head nails. Needlework, of course, went out of style for furniture about 1770 in England (with exceptions). In the Colonies this fashion edict was more or less ignored, and the ladies stitched on. Some of Chippendale's Chinese chairs had cane seats on which a cushion was placed.

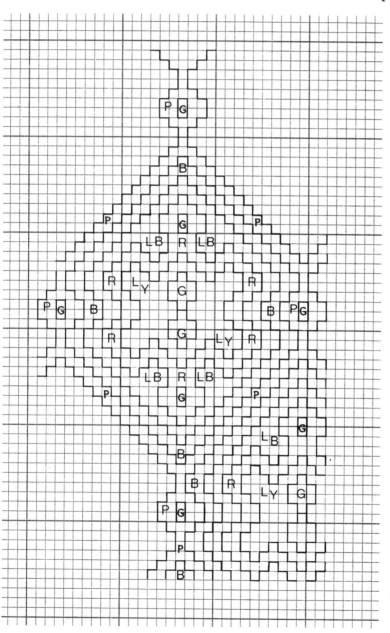

Geometric brick stitch pattern, adapted from an example from the second half of the eighteenth century.

Sample of brick stitch geometric pattern worked in silks on linen. Suitable for upholstery, ca. 1750–1770. See Plate 12 for an adaptation using the original colors but slightly reduced to keep the scale small. Photo: Philip L. Coltrain.

He favored lacquering for this style, which he thought was appropriate for the bedroom. Some feel that his ribband-back chairs with straight legs are his best as far as scale and harmony are concerned.

Straight-legged ladder-back chairs with a prtezel-like pierced twist in the center of each strip are attributed to Chippendale late in his career. Chippendale settees are similar to the chairs; they have double or triple backs joined together at the shoulders. His sofas, with their out-curving, upholstered arms and serpentine or camel-humped backs, were a great favorite in the United States. The legs are either straight or cabriole; the visible wood is held to a minimum. They are not typically upholstered in needlework. Chippendale wing chairs may be identified by their ball-and-claw feet if the legs are cabriole, or if they are straight by the little cock beading on them. The cabriole leg is slightly heavier

Chippendale-style sofa, Philadelphia, ca. 1770.

Chippendale-style bench.

Chippendale "French"
armchair, 1760–1765.

than the Queen Anne leg. The leading edge of the wing is often upholstered to the outside edge of the wing instead of banded as in the
Queen Anne style.

In the Colonies the Chippendale chair was again regionalized so
that experts can tell from the ornamentation of the splat the area in

Chippendale ribbon-back settee, ca. 1755. Part of a set of four matching chairs. Note the tape around the edge of the upholstery. Victoria and Albert Museum. Crown Copyright.

Design motifs: patera, guilloche.

Philadelphia armchair in the Queen
Anne style but made between 1740 and
1760. Though the form of the chair
adheres to the Queen Anne style,
its elegance and enriched lines indicate
a later date. The needlework is not
original to the chair but is attractive
nevertheless. Courtesy of the Museum
of Fine Arts, Houston, the Bayou
Bend Collection.

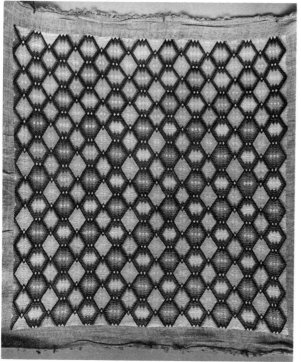

Chair seat, Irish stitch on linen,
ca. 1750, English. Victoria
and Albert Museum. Crown
Copyright.

Transitional side chair, one of a set of four. This chair has the characteristics of both Queen Anne (solid splat, trifid feet) and Chippendale (crested top rail) and thus is called Transitional. Mrs. Philip Bonsal, a talented needlewoman, worked four chair seats in bargello patterns using just one color of wool. To show off the texture and to accent the design she also used the half cross-stitch and the Gobelin stitch. From the collection of the Honorable and Mrs. Philip Bonsal. Photo: Bonnie Boyle.

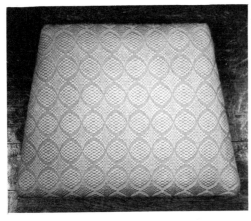

Slip seat for Transitional chair designed and worked by Mrs. Philip Bonsal in gold-colored wool. Half cross-stitch was used to outline the bargello pattern. From the collection of the Honorable and Mrs. Philip Bonsal. Photo: Bonnie Boyle.

which it was made. The typical cupid's-bow back with pierced splat was the American favorite, followed by the ribband back. The Gothic style evidently did not appeal to our simpler tastes or less skilled country craftsmen.

The cabinetmaker or upholsterer was not just a maker of chairs and chests in the eighteenth century. He was also a designer and a co-ordinator of other craftsmen. Today we might describe such a person as a decorator. This title fits Chippendale and his work—he was an arbiter of taste. It is thought that Chippendale himself only designed furniture but did not actually make it. He had several quite excellent designers working with him as well as many fine craftsmen. His book

Slip seat of the Transitional chair at Gunston Hall. The background is blackish brown, the square frame is in shades of gold, and the fruits are in warm shades of red, yellow, green, and blue. Courtesy of the Board of Regents, Gunston Hall Plantation, Lorton, Virginia. Photo: Bonnie Boyle.

Transitional chair with needlepoint slip seat. This chair is in the Palladian room of Gunston Hall Plantation, the home of George Mason in Lorton, Virginia. The needlepoint, though not original to the chair, is believed to be contemporaneous. It was probably cut down from a larger piece. Note the scallop shell on the crest of the chair and the trifid feet echoing the carving on the ears of the crest. Courtesy of the Board of Regents, Gunston Hall Plantation, Lorton, Virginia. Photo: Bonnie Boyle.

Country Chippendale side chair, cherry, mid-eighteenth century. Note the perfect cupid's-bow crest on the back contrasting with the otherwise straight and sturdy lines of the rest of the chair. See Plate 10 for the orginal seat of the chair. Courtesy of the Connecticut Historical Society, Hartford, Connecticut.

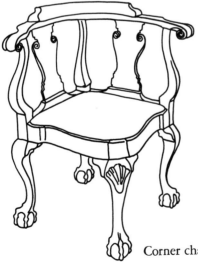

Corner chair, mid-eighteenth century, Philadelphia.

was a masterful piece of advertising. Robert Manwaring, William Ince, and Thomas Mayhew published later, but similar, pattern books. These books were invaluable to the American furniture makers. In America the upholsterer had even more duties to perform for the public than just making furniture and purveying materials. He was also a supplier of Venetian blinds, and he sold and hung wallpaper.

In 1738 word of new excavations at Herculaneum and Pompeii reached the world. The discoveries of whole rooms buried for centuries fascinated everyone, but it was not until 1760 that these excavations affected the world of decoration. When they did, they affected it profoundly. People had had enough of the rather sybaritic life, represented by the French court at least, and wished to return to the virtues they thought the ancient Greeks and Romans represented. The change evolved slowly, and it was not until the turn of the century that early Greek and Roman furniture styles were actually copied. From 1760 on, the symbols of ancient times were absorbed into the decorators' catalogs and combined with symbols of the present. The drawings of Piranesi were a great source of inspiration to designers and decorators, Robert Adam being one of them.

Design motifs: arabesque, acanthus leaf.

Robert Adam was the second complete decorator in Georgian times chronologically but not in sphere of influence. Refined elegance was the keynote of his decorating credo. Colors lost their intensity in his hands; furniture became more space than substance. Balance, line, and detail were his hallmarks. His attention to detail was so great that he designed the moldings and hardware, even the carpets, for the homes on which he worked. The molding on the wall dado matched the carving on the furniture placed in front of it.

After studying in Italy, Adam rose within two or three years of his return to England to be the sole architect to King George III, who ascended the throne in 1760. After Adam held this position for a few years, his brother James replaced him so that he could attend to their thriving business. Whereas before, walls had been covered with wood or fabric, Adam preferred to cover them with plaster or stucco with delicately painted decoration. Angelica Kauffmann designed ceilings and panels for him, introducing a note of softness to the classical world that was her subject matter. Adam favored the oval shape for decoration, though his furniture tended to be more angular. The decoration of the furniture was not allowed to overpower its lines. Such men as Chippendale, Hepplewhite, and Sheraton drew on Adam's furniture designs for inspiration.

Adam-style armchair.

Though bolder shades of blue retained their popularity, all other colors faded to pastel. Adam liked pale pink, green, lavender, and blue. His furniture was often painted, sometimes the same color as the room. The idea was to blend the furniture with the rest of the decoration of the room. Satinwood lent itself to his lighter furniture, though mahogany was still used. The cabriole leg went out of style, to be replaced by a straighter leg with fluting or stringing in a contrasting color of wood. Adam chair backs have no distinctive shape recognizable at a glance as a Queen Anne or Chippendale chair does. The backs may be oval, straight, shield-like, or serpentine; their only common characteristic is their fineness of line and proportion.

Tapestry, either French or English, was used for upholstery. Silk with scattered sprigs of flowers, leather, and horsehair were used too. Embroidery was used sparingly. Adam designed a rather distinctive window seat with out-curving arms and no back. It was upholstered, with wood showing only on the legs.

Favorite Adam decorations included delicate swags of flowers, tall tripod urns, lunettes with radiating rays, medallions of classical figures, and the lyre. Wedgwood plaques and medallions often adorned furniture made to an Adam design. Adam's impact was slight in the Colonies, partly because during his heyday the colonists were otherwise occupied with more important matters, such as a revolution, and partly because Adam's book *Works of Architecture* (1773) had so few actual furniture patterns to copy.

The neoclassical style brought about a change in French furniture too, but not quite as much as in England. Light colors and a penchant for delicate swags of flowers had already become fashionable before Adam. The cabriole leg was no longer in style but was succeeded by a straight leg that sprang from a square attached to the seat. The square was usually decorated with a rosette. The legs were usually tapered down to the ankle with fluting or were of a vase-like shape. The upholstery was boxed up from the seat rail. The back of the chair might have an upholstered oval set between two straight uprights. Lyre backs were popular too. A new style of stool was made in which a boxed cushion rested in a frame supported by straight but tapered legs. Tapestry showing animals of the hunt covered such cushions; roses trimmed

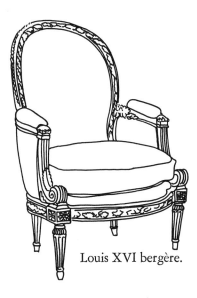

Louis XVI bergère.

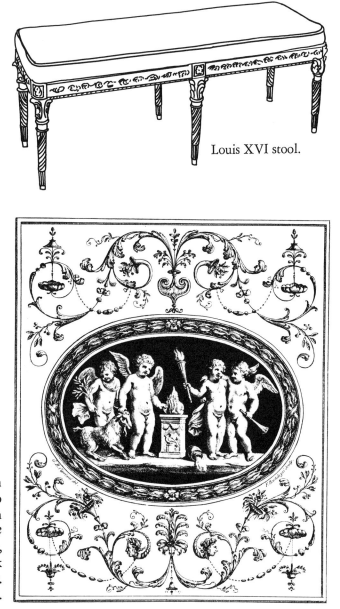

Louis XVI stool.

Neoclassical ornament design
by Michelangelo Pergolesi, who
worked with Robert Adam in
London. From *Classical Ornament
of the Eighteenth Century*,
a collection of Pergolesi's work
compiled by Edward A. Maser.
Photo: Philip L. Coltrain.

Late Louis XIV side chair. The back of the chair is decorated with a balloon, an object of great interest in Europe in the late 1780s. It is not known whether the seat (shown in Plate 15) is original to the chair or not. Nevertheless, it is an excellent example of capitalizing on a prominent decorative feature of the chair for the design of the upholstery. The tulip border is a subtle reminder of another mania, tulip mania, which possessed Europe in the 1630s. Courtesy of the Air and Space Museum of the Smithsonian Institution, Washington, D.C., Gift of Mr. and Mrs. William A. M. Burden.

the boxed borders. Round stools with squat little legs were also made.

The paintings of Jean-Honoré Fragonard best exemplify the essence of the period in decoration, all phases reflecting sweetness, light, and charm.

Dainty silks were specially woven to fit the backs and seats of chairs. A typical motif was a basket of flowers surrounded by a wavy ribbon border. Similar designs were worked in needlepoint, often done en suite for canapés, bergères and chauffeuses (side chairs). A set worked for Malmaison showed swags of flowers framing roses, with ribbons joining the swags to each other, all very delicate and sweet. Silk embroidery on silk, often showing the owner's monogram, was placed on the back of chairs. It is said that Marie Antoinette had such a chair. Striped silks with flowers in stripes and plain silks with sprigs of flowers on a white or pastel background were considered very styl-

Silk and silver thread embroidery on silk satin, possibly a petticoat panel of Austrian or southern French origin, included because it illustrates some of the decorative motifs of the second half of the eighteenth century. Courtesy of the Indianapolis Museum of Art, Gift of Mr. and Mrs. W. J. Holliday, Sr.

Louis XVI canapé matching the bergère pictured in Plate 14. Courtesy of the Honorable and Mrs. Marion Smoak. Photo: Bonnie Boyle.

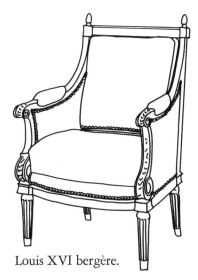

Louis XVI bergère.

ish. The sprigged silks had a greater amount of open space and were copied for printed cottons in England and in the country that was France's new ally, America. The silks also made their impression on crewel designs in America. The floral sprays worked in the late eighteenth century have a less naïve look to them.

Velvets with allover geometric patterns, damasks, brocades, and moirés were used. Lampas with scenes in red, yellow, and green were popular for a while; then ivory became the favorite color. Beauvais tapestries woven to fit particular chairs depicted pastoral scenes with no border or frame; the simple trim on the chairs was made to serve as the frame. Toile de Jouy, still a great favorite today, was first printed by Christopher-Philippe Oberkampf at Jouy in 1760. At first toile was printed in deep rose on a natural or light background. The designs were of peasants and aristocracy in bucolic settings. Later designs were of a more patriotic nature; some were commemorative of great national events.

Because Louis XVI was more interested in mechanical things and less interested in the arts than his predecessors, fewer radical changes in decoration took place during his reign. The middle class in both England and France was able to afford and took a greater interest in

Crewel design adapted from Indian chintz, last quarter of the eighteenth century.

interior decoration; consequently, more different types of furniture were made and for different purposes. Symmetry again became the order of the day with the increased interest in Roman architecture. Sèvres porcelain plaques were set into furniture in a fashion similar to the English Wedgwood. Roman friezes or grisaille ornamented walls and, in miniature, the backs of chairs. Grisaille is imitation bas-relief panels painted in monotone showing classical figures in tableaux. Caryatids decorated the same piece of furniture as a pair of doves and a basket of flowers, with no thought of the incongruity. Chinoiserie, floral swags, and laurel wreaths might appear together on another piece. Jean-Henri Riesener, a German who moved to France, and Martin Carlin, of German origin but French nationality, are considered two of the greatest cabinetmakers

Crewel design adapted from American crewel valance, last quarter of the eighteenth century. Courtesy of Benjamin Ginsburg, Antiquary, New York.

A Louis XVI fire screen that once belonged to Marie Antoinette. Note the delicate carving on the frame. This screen was included because it is a good example of chinoiserie needlework. The needlework is not original to the screen and might even be from an earlier period. From the collection of the Honorable and Mrs. Philip Bonsal. Photo: Bonnie Boyle.

of Louis XVI's reign. Boulard, Jean-Baptise Lelarge, and Foliot were well known for their chairs.

The best known of the late eighteenth-century English designers were George Hepplewhite and Thomas Sheraton. They interpreted in their own way the designs of Adam, neoclassicism, and French fashion. They, in turn, greatly influenced the furniture of America through their pattern books.

Little is known about George Hepplewhite, the man. His pattern book, *The Cabinet Maker and Upholsterer's Guide*, was published posthumously by his widow in 1788. It is thought to be a compilation of his contemporaries' designs, the same thing said of Chippendale's book. The essence of Hepplewhite's style was noted in the preface to his book where he stated that he wished to combine elegance and utility.

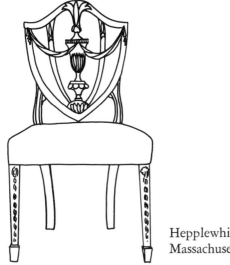

Hepplewhite side chair,
Massachusetts, ca. 1780.

The classic Hepplewhite chair has a shield back and straight legs tapering down to spade feet. A delicate inlay may decorate the back of the chair and the legs. The front of the upholstered seat might be curved. However, there are variations: heart-shaped and square-backed side chairs, ladder backs similar to Chippendale's, fluted or reeded legs, even an occasional cabriole leg on French-influenced chairs. The variations retain the delicacy of inlay in ovals, squares, and circles on the back of the chair. Stringing was a characteristic decoration on the legs. Though Hepplewhite rarely showed intricate carving, he was the first to use the classic three-feathers motif of the Prince of Wales. The typical Hepplewhite sofa has straight legs with an in-curving wooden arm starting from the leg. The arm eases into a slightly curved upholstered back. There is a curve to the front of the seat. As in the case of Chippendale, there is no authenticated furniture attributed to Hepplewhite as craftsman.

The preferred upholstery materials for Hepplewhite were tapestry, plain or striped horsehair, figured silks and satins, and leather for dining-room chairs. The colors used were pale, even cream and white, and some red or blue damask was used. Striped satin and watered silks as well as Spitalfields silk made in England were popular too. The

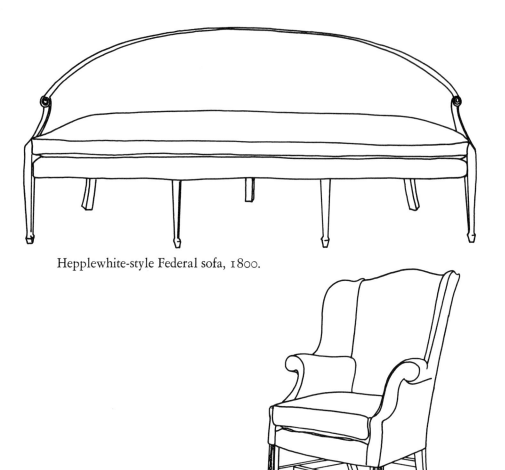

Hepplewhite-style Federal sofa, 1800.

Hepplewhite-style wing chair, Philadelphia.

English silks featured some chinoiserie patterns with light backgrounds at that time. The chairs were sometimes gilded or japanned.

As mentioned before, a wing chair of the Hepplewhite style can be distinguished from one of an earlier period by the arm treatment. A Hepplewhite wing springs from the arm, which starts from the back of the chair. There is usually more curve to the wing. Hepplewhite recommended that wing chairs be upholstered in horsehair or leather or that a slipcase be made to put over the original canvas (now muslin) covering.

Needlepoint seat made for a Hepplewhite chair in the French style. The background is light blue. Courtesy of Benjamin Ginsburg, Antiquary, New York. Photo: Helga Photo Studio.

Thomas Sheraton published *The Cabinet-Maker and Upholsterer's Drawing-Book* over a period of several years, from 1791 to 1794, and the *Cabinet Dictionary* in 1803. The small craftsman shop was disappearing in favor of a type of manufacturing resembling factory work and there was a need for good pattern books. Surprisingly, Sheraton barely made a living from his books, and no known example of his own cabinetwork exists; nevertheless, he made a great impact on furniture design. In America, Allison, Lannuier, and especially Samuel McIntire of Salem relied heavily on his design books.

The typical early Sheraton side chair has a rectangular back as opposed to the curved back of Hepplewhite. The legs of the chair taper; he preferred round legs with fluting or spiral turning. Sofas had straight legs with wooden arms rising over the legs and curving up to a flat

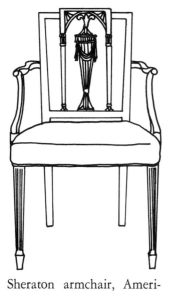

Sheraton armchair, American, ca. 1800.

Drawing-room chair design from *The Cabinet-Maker and Upholsterer's Drawing-Book* by Thomas Sheraton. This illustrates the type of design Sheraton thought appropriate for upholstery. Photo: Philip L. Coltrain.

Sheraton-style sofa, Massachusetts, ca. 1800.

wood crested back crowned in the center with carving. Some settees were made by both designers of the joined chair back style.

Sheraton loved symbolism. His books explained the symbolism for each ornament in the designs. This sat very well with his American copiers, who adopted some of the French revolutionary symbols and added to them the eagle. His early chair backs were very light and airy with delicate carving as ornament. His sense of proportion was acute. However, his later designs coarsened and became almost vulgar in their excessive use of ornament.

Ornament for a frieze or tablet from *The Cabinet-Maker and Upholsterer's Drawing-Book* by Thomas Sheraton. The creature is a griffin with an arabesque tail. Photo: Philip L. Coltrain.

Various styles of acanthus leaves from *The Cabinet-Maker and Upholsterer's Drawing-Book* by Thomas Sheraton. Photo: Philip L. Coltrain.

Repeat pattern, English, ca. 1790.

He seemed to like silks and satins as chair coverings, mentioning in one design a panel of printed silk appliquéd to a chair back pad. The panel had a plain border, and plain matching fabric was used on the seat. Some designs show grisaille-like decoration on the upholstery, whether embroidered or printed it is hard to tell. It is safe to say that needlepoint is not the most appropriate covering for Sheraton chairs, nor is crewel. However, needlepoint in small diaper patterns was used on cabriolet chairs using Sheraton designs. Silk embroidery or, as

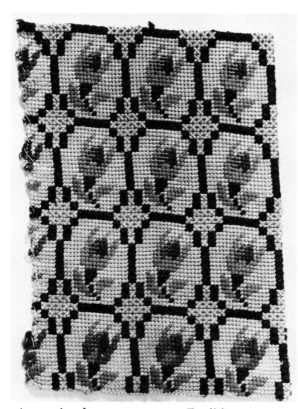

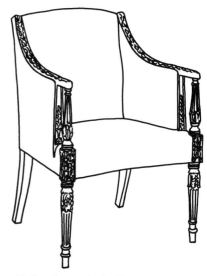

A sample of a repeat pattern, English, ca. 1790. The rosebuds are framed in black worked in Smyrna cross-stitch. The background is a pale fawn. See page 112 for the graph.

Federal armchair, Sheraton type.

mentioned, a panel of figured silk with a simple border would seem to be in keeping with his ideas. Some embroidery was done on satin with silk at that time, but much of this fragile work has disappeared and it is hard to determine how popular it was. It still exists in pole screens because Sheraton recommended covering it with glass.

Some of Sheraton's furniture had inlay and some, like that of Hepplewhite, was gilded. Sheraton seemed to prefer to gild over white paint. Some of his designs show banister backs. One thing peculiar to both Sheraton and Hepplewhite is that the design on the chair back does not touch the chair seat as does the center splat of Queen Anne and Chippendale chairs. Sheraton wing chairs are very much like Hepplewhite's except that they are apt to have rounded legs and no

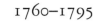
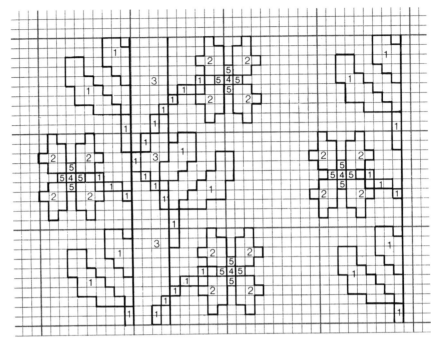

Hepplewhite-type stripe pattern.

stretchers. Tub chairs or, as they were called, gondola chairs had straight tapered legs, either round or square. Late in his career Sheraton's furniture adopted some of the French Directoire style with outscrolled arms and legs and more horizontal lines.

American furniture at the time of Sheraton and Hepplewhite is called Federal after the establishment of the American government in 1789. Before that American furniture is referred to as Colonial. Walnut and mahogany were the chief woods used for eighteenth-century chairs and carving was the usual decoration, gilding seldom being done. Japanning was popular, as evidenced by many advertisements in the Northern newspapers. After the Revolution more fabrics were imported, and the use of needlework and woolen cloth or woolen mixes diminished. Lampas (a patterned silk), painted silks, silk damasks and brocades, and chintzes were imported. Satins, damasks, or taberays (a striped silk) were favored for the dining room. Cotton prints were used en suite, which was the style for other fabrics too. Horsehair, and something called satin horsehair, Russia leather, and morocco leather in red, yellow, and green were used. For chairs with a cane seat made from the middle of the eighteenth century into the early nineteenth century, it is appropriate to use a boxed cushion. It can be piped or corded on the edges and should be fairly firm.

MOTIFS

England	America	France
Chippendale	Eagle heads	Lyres
Dragons	Tassels	La Fontaine tales
Long-legged birds	Local flora	Grisaille
Bamboo	and fauna	Running frets
Pagodas	Shells	Natural flowers in
Chinese frets	Paterae	garlands, swags, and
Rocks and trees in	Anthemions	festoons
oriental style		Eagles
Gothic forms, cusps,		Rams
lancets, crockets,		Sphinxes
trefoils, and cinque-		Dolphins
foils		Griffins
Guilloches		Bowknots and inter-
Ovals		laced ribbons
Paterae		Roses, daisies, and
Ribbons		chrysanthemum-like
Flowers in vases		flowers tied with
Geometrics		trailing ribbon
Acanthus leaves		Pompeiian arabesques
Drapery and tassels		Pastoral figures
		Wheat sheaves
		Cupids and bows
		Trophies of love and
		farming
		Birds
		Moths
		Butterflies
		Acanthus leaf bands
		Fluted columns

MOTIFS
Adam-Hepplewhite-Sheraton

England	*America*
Wheat ears	Festoons of bellflowers and
Bellflowers in drops and swags	husks
Swags of leaves combined with	Rosettes
caryatids	Paterae
Paterae	Simply framed figures of Justice
Ribbons	or Temperance
Shields	Cornucopias
Prince of Wales feathers	Eagles
Vases and urns	Stars
Anthemions	Draperies
Ram heads	Pastoral scenes
Winged griffins	Natural flowers
Festoons of drapery	Lunettes
Grotesques	
Natural flowers à la Angelica	
Kauffmann	
Gods and heroes such as	
Mercury, Psyche, Cupid,	
and Achilles	
Eggs and darts	
Flowers spilling out of baskets	
Lunettes	

CHAPTER EIGHT

1795-1805

The severe and simple lines of Greek and Roman furniture were infinitely more in keeping with the mood of the French people than the furniture in style before the French Revolution. Even the color scheme changed. Gone were the pale shades, and in came vigorous colors such as bottle green, mulberry, eggplant (aubergine), and golden yellow. Striped multicolor silks and horsehair replaced the delicate flower sprigs, though floral stripes did not go out of fashion entirely during the days of the Republic.

Jacques Louis David was the designer and arbiter of taste for the Directoire period. He was an extremely skilled painter, a true Republican, a member of the National Convention, and also a designer of some talent. He espoused fairly undiluted Greek styles of furniture and decoration. The klismos was the form on which Directoire chairs are modeled. Elements of the klismos are found in chairs throughout the neoclassical and Empire periods. The concave back line with the rolled-over top rail and saber-like front legs was the standard. Variations were made in the front legs, giving them a vase shape, and in the back with upholstery or a single elegant splat. Bold line and symmetry were the keynotes. The chairs were not heavy-looking. What decoration they bore was kept within the basic outline of the chair. If the chair had arms, they flowed in an easy curve from the back right over the upright supports, which rose directly over the front legs. Arm pads were still used but not as generously as before. The upholstery was attached with brass tacks and sometimes trimmed with tape.

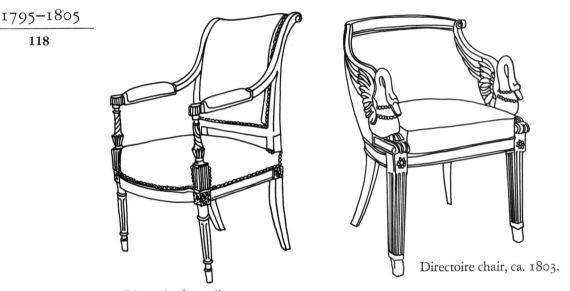

Directoire chair, ca. 1803.

Directoire fauteuil, ca. 1795.

Another style of chair with origins in the past was a barrel-like one with great swan shapes forming the arms, the wings sweeping up to the straight but semicircular back. The front legs were rather heavy and fluted; the back legs were somewhat splayed out and square. The upholstery material was always plain, but the urge to gild died hard even with the new Republic. Thus the swan arms or perhaps an entire chair shone with gold.

In England, Hepplewhite and Sheraton styles coexisted with the Greco-Roman styles of the classical revival. The Prince of Wales had not yet assumed the regency for his father, George III, and so busied himself with improving his residences, particularly Carlton House. He was aided in this project by Henry Holland and later Walsh Porter. Holland's taste was classical but opulent. He liked heavy draperies, gilded molding on the walls, and simulated marble columns and door frames called scagliola. (By mixing plaster of Paris with color and bits of marble, an imitation of any kind or color of marble could be painted.) Holland was also fond of the Louis XVI style and interpreted it in his own way for the prince.

In America the Directoire style was taken up by Duncan Phyfe,

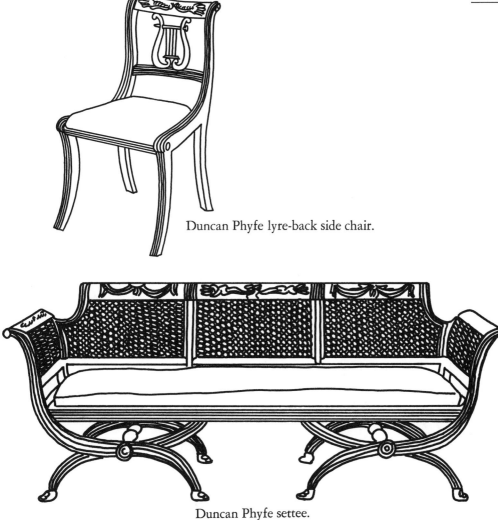

Duncan Phyfe lyre-back side chair.

Duncan Phyfe settee.

though in point of time this style occurred a few years later than in France. Phyfe particularly liked the lyre motif—to Americans it is almost an identifying mark of his style. This period is considered by some to be his best work as his handling of proportion and details became coarser in later years. Other Phyfe style characteristics are the use of fluting, coiled or volute chair arms, and curved X-shaped legs on both chairs and settees. Phyfe furniture has more of a horizontal than vertical line, a sweeping graceful flow.

Other furniture makers in America were making more upright and square-backed chairs, with a predilection for attaching the upholstery with brass nail heads in straight and scalloped rows. The legs were often straight or slightly splayed out, the backs delicately carved in a shield shape or accented with three or four slender pillars. Settees and armchairs were made in the same style, light but well proportioned. This furniture was sometimes trimmed with bellflowers down the legs and on the back. It was often painted white or a light color with fine foliage overpainted on the chair rail, the back, and the legs.

A suite of furniture attributed to Duncan Phyfe in the classical style (also known as the French Restoration style), ca. 1837. The furniture is mahogany veneer. The upholstery is a copy of the original linen and wool material; the colors are crimson and gold. Note the border on the raised portion of the gondola chairs, the méridienne, and the tabourets. Courtesy of the Metropolitan Museum of Art, Purchase, Gift of L. E. Katzenbach, 1966.

Martha Washington chair, ca. 1790.

This lightness prevailed in easy chairs, which were of the Hepplewhite style but almost too insubstantial. A popular form of upholstered chair was a barrel-backed type of bergère. The whole chair was framed in wood with a covering of plain fabric or leather. This might be what was called a French elbow chair in a 1798 newspaper advertisement. Lolling or Martha Washington chairs with straight, high-rising backs and open wooden arms were also fashionable.

In a Charleston paper in 1798 William Cocks advertised Windsor chairs "in all colors" as well as French-back stools and cabriolets. Thus it would appear that French influence was strong at least in the South. The advertisement mentioned that satins and brocades were on the chairs already made.

MOTIFS

France	*America*
Tricolor cockades	Lyres
Swans	Eagles
Dolphins	Stars
Lyres	Bellflowers in chains
Drums	Torches and quivers of arrows
Trumpets	Paterae
Spears	Moths
Pikes as symbol of freedom of man	Simple vases of flowers
	Conch shells
Clasped hands—fraternity	Pastoral scenes
Eye in triangle—reason	Rosettes
Spade topped by Phrygian bonnet	Swags of drapery
	Swags of flowers held up by ribbons
Stars	Classical figures, often seated
Liberty caps	Roses
Palm leaves	
Papyrus flowers	
Lotuses	
Caryatids	
Daisies	
Lunettes	

CHAPTER NINE

1805-1830

The Empire style in France was as bold as the new Emperor Napoleon. The principles of Greco-Roman classical design remained, but the new version was much more straightforward and robust than Directoire furniture. Napoleon's campaign in Egypt added another source of decorative motif to the ones already current. This decoration took the form of carvings touched with gilt and brass mounts applied to the surface of the wood or inlaid. Previously the metal ornaments covered a joint or served some useful purpose; they now existed for decoration only. The edges of Empire furniture were squared and sharp, but because of the curve of the back and legs it escaped the boxy look. The front legs on armchairs were often columnar in shape with Egyptian decoration, or they might have a caryatid at the top and an animal foot at the bottom.

David continued in favor with Napoleon. For the redecoration of Malmaison he appointed Charles Percier and Pierre Fontaine as his architects. They also worked at the Tuileries and the Louvre. They designed furniture and interiors as their predecessors had done before the Revolution. The result was a slightly more sparing use of decoration of a more substantial character, and again symmetry was important.

Upholstery fabrics were compatible with the new fashion in furniture, the brighter colors requiring that the designs be less intricate. They were, however, by no means simple. Silk brocades were still

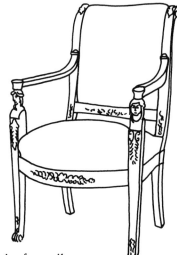

French Empire fauteuil.

woven to fit a specific style of chair, but the floral designs consisted of larger shapes without ribbons and swags. Damasks were woven with strong two-color patterns. Stripes alternating with a pattern and plain fields with medallions were among the favored styles. Some damask was woven in just one color, the weave showing off the design that might be Egyptian in derivation. Velvets with applied gimp or embroidery added elegance. Napoleon was not averse to having his initial used as the chief motif on upholstery. Horsehair, striped silks with rather narrow stripes, plain silks, and leather were the more sedate materials used. Toiles commemorating the Republic and Napoleon were popular. Favorite colors during this period were wine red, royal purple, yellow, and emerald green.

After the restoration of the monarchy in France, the lines of the Empire style were simplified appreciably and decoration was refined, resulting in a heavier look than before. Columns were used for supports for sofa arms, desk fronts, and tables. The single scroll was the other main element of design introduced; it was used to form arms of chairs, table legs, and shelf supports. French furniture after the Empire became more a mixture of styles and less trend-setting. Old styles were revived, given some new features, and eagerly taken up by

French Empire damask stripe, ca. 1810. Courtesy of Benjamin Ginsburg, Antiquary, New York.

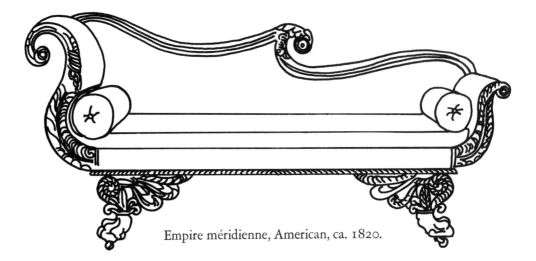

Empire méridienne, American, ca. 1820.

the Americans. The impression one gets of upholstery fabrics is that velvets, stripes, and damasks (both symmetrical and asymmetrical) never went out of style.

The Empire style was greatly appreciated in America, so much so that this period is called American Empire. It lasted considerably longer than it did in France, or at least the American interpretation did. A little more carved decoration was used on side chairs in particular, and the lines seemed to soften somewhat. As mentioned before, Duncan Phyfe was one of the great designers of this period. Other designers were Charles-Honoré Lannuier and Anthony G. Quervelle. The very late American Empire furniture became more bulky-looking and was more heavily decorated with carving; this is particularly true of sofas. The lines were horizontal with long, level backs, out-turned arms, and curving feet often in the shape of a dolphin or cornucopia. During the late Empire period another style competed with it, called the classical or "pillar and scroll" style, the American version of the French Restoration style. The heaviness in Empire style increased in the classical style. All decoration was reduced to the scroll and the pillar with perhaps a little gilt collar on the pillar. Veneers were used over simpler woods on the larger pieces such as couches and sofas.

A popular side chair was called a gondola chair; it had saber legs and a klismos yoke with a vase-shaped splat to the seat. The uprights

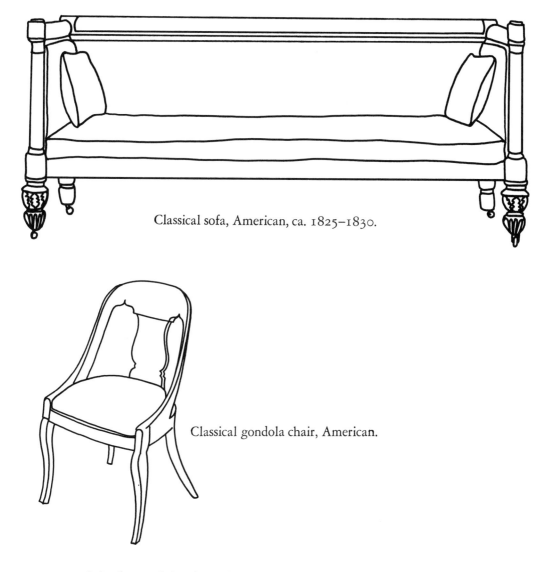

Classical sofa, American, ca. 1825–1830.

Classical gondola chair, American.

swept toward the front of the chair. A slip seat was used. Sometimes the shoulders of the yoke were rounded. Armchairs in this style had large scrolls for arms, which were placed over the front legs. The distinctive thing about the upholstery was that it was often boxed, so that the leading edge bore an elaborate border in contrast to a plain seat. Sometimes the seat had a single round damask medallion on it.

Empire furniture in America was upholstered with the same types of fabric used in France except for tapestry. Horsehair woven with various warps and wefts such as silk, wool, or cotton was used. Geometric patterns were woven into the horsehair which was a solid color. Stripes in silks and damasks with large gold medallions on them were considered very grand. In a letter to her daughter Madame Jumel of New York mentioned a rich yellow satin with medallions. Red, especially for dining rooms, was a favorite color; blue green was another.

A great number of fancy or side chairs were manufactured in America during this period. The basic line was that of a klismos with saber legs, a rolled-over back, and if not a hard wood seat, a slip seat. The back rail might be painted, but it was usually plain with a second rail underneath it highly carved in silhouette. The front feet sometimes terminated in hairy dog paws. Another variation had two plain back rails with an eagle or lyre stretched between them. Some fancy chairs had klismos tops and Sheraton-type legs with stretchers added. These chairs have a heavier appearance and are quite often painted all over with considerable gilt decoration. Knife-edged cushions tied on with tassels are appropriate for the classic style, minus the tassels for the Sheraton leg style.

Classical armchair, American, 1835.

Empire fancy chair,
American, ca. 1825.

Fancy chair,
American, ca. 1830.

The fancy chair never really went out of style. Lambert Hitchcock added a further variation in his chair factory in Connecticut. His chairs had straight legs or slightly splayed front legs, separated by stretchers. The slightly rolled back had three rails, and the seat was rush. The most distinctive features of his chairs were that they were painted black and the center rail of the back was stenciled in color and gilt. The stencils were usually of fruit or foliage. Hitchcock made many variations of the fancy chair. Some chairs have a sausage-like center on the top rail; others might have an eagle silhouetted and painted on the center back rail. Other manufacturers made other designs with solid seats, rounded top yokes, and highly turned legs, but they all come under the name of fancy chair. Tied-on chair pads are appropriate for them all, nineteenth-century patterned needlepoint being the best choice for embroidery.

It was in 1803 that the beginnings of a new trend in needlework started. An engraver and landscape painter named A. Philipson published a pattern book in Berlin. The unique thing about the pattern book was that the patterns were printed on checkered paper with a different symbol in the outside outline of each color. The colors were then painted in by hand, square by square. To the needleworker each square represented a stitch. The book showed patterns of bouquets,

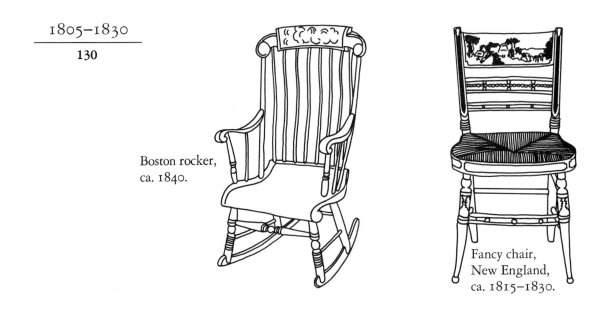

Boston rocker,
ca. 1840.

Fancy chair,
New England,
ca. 1815–1830.

Fancy chair with chair pad
worked by the foster daughter
of George Washington, Nellie
Custis Lewis. The wreath design
on a white background is worked
in cross-stitch. Courtesy of the
Woodlawn Plantation, a property
of the National Trust for
Historic Preservation. Photo:
Bonnie Boyle.

Berlin pattern, first half of the nineteenth century. Photo: Philip L. Coltrain.

garlands, arabesques, vases, and landscapes. Another Berliner, Frau Wittich, took up the idea and soon led the market in printed patterns. The patterns were called Berlin patterns and were the main feature of a fad called Berlin work that soon swept Europe and America.

The English had previously provided the Continent with embroidery wool, crewels, and a heavy worsted. The popularity of Berlin patterns created a demand for a larger color range and a wool finer than worsted but as soft as crewel. The German production of merino wool grew to meet this demand, and the wool was named Berlin wool. Cotton production also increased at the turn of the century in part because of increased importation from the United States and also because of improved processing machinery. An evenly woven open canvas was developed around the 1820s. The best came from France and England. Soon pattern making was carried on in other German cities, France, and Holland. Because of the industrial revolution, the middle-class housewife had fewer necessities to manufacture at home and thus had more time for embroidery. Thus all the ingredients came together at the same time to lay the groundwork for an international mania. Pillows, seat

Berlin pattern, Empire style, ca. 1810.

coverings, rugs, pole screens, pictures, footstool covers, and even upholstery for sofas were covered in Berlin work.

At first the patterns were worked with silk or wool on fine silk
canvas, and the background was left bare. A piece of colored silk was
placed behind it to give the proper "effect." Cotton canvas, being
cheaper, soon replaced the silk and backgrounds were filled in. Light
colors such as white, tan, and blue were favorites. It was only after 1850
that the very dark colors, including black, were used for backgrounds.
The colors were quite vivid even before the advent of aniline dyes
around 1860. Mauve and magenta were the first of the anilines. Subject
matter for the patterns expanded to include the British royal family,
religious subjects, and copies of the works of famous painters such as
Sir Edwin Landseer. Because it was a sentimental age, some of the subject matter is rather cloying. Border patterns of foliage and flowers

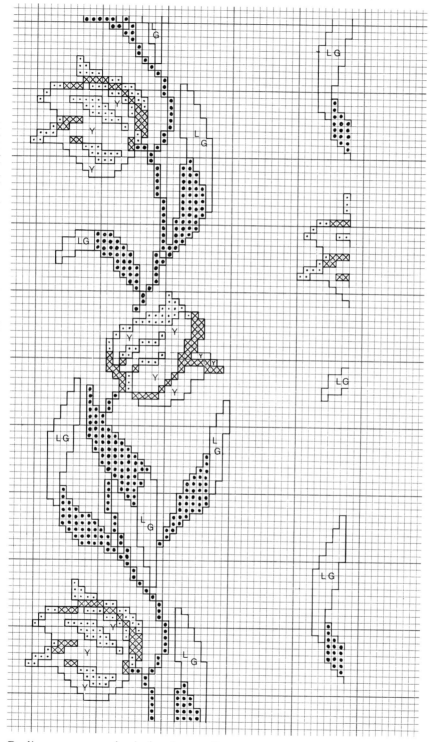

Berlin pattern, neoclassical style, ca. 1805.

were quite popular and rather pretty. The fad lasted from about 1830 to the 1860s in England and about ten to fifteen years longer in America and France. Magazines started printing patterns about 1860. Other forms of embroidery were done, but Berlin work dominated the field.

The idea of appliquéing needlework to another ground was revived from the seventeenth century. Large patterns were worked and then sewn to dark-colored broadcloth. Cording was sewn about the edges to tidy up the outline. Another technique was to baste canvas over broadcloth or horsehair (and a fine lining material under that) and then work the pattern through the three layers. When the work was completed, the canvas threads were raveled close to the work and the canvas threads were then pulled out one by one, leaving only the pattern sitting up on the grounds. Both techniques were used for upholstery.

Aside from Regency furniture (and there are exceptions here too),

Cushion, silk on canvas, cross-stitch, English, mid-nineteenth century. Made by Mary Anne Redfern. Victoria and Albert Museum. Crown Copyright.

Berlin woolwork made about 1848 by Anne Redfern of Cambridge, England. Victoria and Albert Museum. Crown Copyright.

Classical-style footstool with appliquéd needlepoint upholstery. Nellie Custis Lewis, the foster daughter of George Washington, worked the charming puppy and butterfly for her grandson. It is beautifully stitched to black wool broadcloth. Courtesy of the Woodlawn Plantation, a property of the National Trust for Historic Preservation. Photo: Bonnie Boyle.

Regency side chair, brass inlay, ca. 1820.

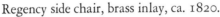

needlepoint is appropriate for nineteenth-century furniture from about 1830 to the 1880s. Bolster cushions are a possible idea for early Empire if the upholstery fabric does not conflict with the needlework design. Knife-edged pillows are a possibility for any period. For furniture dating from after the Civil War in the United States, boxing might be more appropriate.

George IV was more interested in houses and their interiors than any other English king after Henry VIII. He enlarged, built, and redecorated more houses than any monarch since then. His choice of styles changed from the time he was Prince Regent until he reached the throne. Furniture from these two periods is a mélange of styles, an eclectic period—Greco-Roman à la French with a dollop of Gothic. One of the designers of the period, Thomas Hope, wanted style to return to the severity of the bronze furniture that was all that remained in the Greek archaeological digs. His furniture was heavy and uncomfortable-looking in the klismos style. Curule chairs were made too. Another designer, George Smith, agreed in part with Hope but felt that the essence of the style was more important than a slavish imitation. The Greek revolt against the Turks in 1821 and the purchase of the Parthenon marbles by Lord Elgin created more interest in Greek styles.

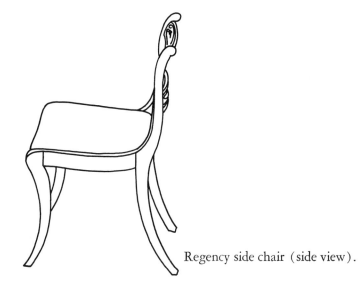

Regency side chair (side view).

Both Hope and Smith used Egyptian ornamentation on their furniture too. Then there was a recurrent interest in things Chinese, and Augustus Pugin revived the Gothic style.

A magazine of the time, Ackerman's *Repository of Arts*, disseminated furniture styles to a larger segment of the public than before. It contained color illustrations of the newest furniture styles and included little swatches of cloth to show the newest colors and fabrics.

The woods used during the Regency period were mahogany, rosewood, and satinwood for the lighter and more delicate furniture. Some soft woods were used and then japanned in black. Metal paw feet were used on tables and chairs. Brass inlays were used on the dark furniture and delicate painting on the satinwood. The ornamentation used during the Pugin Gothic period seems excessive compared with the cleaner lines of the Grecian style. Couches were in the classic style with outcurved arms (one higher than the other), heavy splayed feet, and bolsters tucked in the curve of the arms. Furniture of this period seems either too light or a bit too heavy.

Embroidery used during this period was either silk embroidery on silk or velvet, or the beginnings of the Berlin craze. The Duchess of York worked coverings for chairs and a sofa in needlepoint with spreading baskets of flowers enclosed with borders of leaves as the design. However, her work was the exception, not the rule. Floral damasks in silk, wool, and cotton and chintzes with small floral designs were used. Around 1812 chintz was patterned after damask. In the 1820s columns with florid vines twining around them were roller-printed on cotton. Manchester or cotton velvet was used, as was horsehair. Stripes and moreen were still in style. The delicate-looking furniture was upholstered in appropriately delicate patterned fabrics, the heavier in plain fabrics.

MOTIFS

France

Swans	Victory figures
Winged lions	Chimeras
Caryatids	Laurel wreaths
Sphinxes	Cornucopias
Urns	Spears
Bees	Torches
Helmets	Fasces
Trumpets	Sistrums
Lyres	Paterae
Quivers of arrows	Winged thunderbolts of Jupiter
Anthemions	Gods and goddesses
Acanthus leaves	Rosettes
Palms	Roses
Lotuses	Poppies
Neptune's trident	Initial N
Thyrsus	

England	United States
Swags of flowers	Eagles
Roses	Cornucopias
Swans	Lyres
Caryatids	Fruits
Atlantes	Foliage
Lyres	Eagles with streamers in mouth
Paterae	Stars
Palmettes	Acanthus leaves
Urns	Pineapples
Swags of beading	Lotus flowers
Swags of drapery	Papyrus flowers
Low urns of flowers with melon reeding	Putti in gilt
	Palmettes
Swags of bellflowers	Anthemions
Gods and goddesses in color with simple frame	Dolphins
	Caryatids
Grisaille	Greek keys
Lion heads	Gods and goddesses
Eagle heads	Griffins
Greek keys	
Ram heads	
Winged lions	

CHAPTER TEN

1830-1900

The nineteenth century was the century of revivals, one right after the other and sometimes simultaneously. To delineate the progression of the various revivals in Europe and America would be hopelessly confusing; therefore, we will limit our interest to America and its manufacturers. Classical or Restoration furniture continued in popularity despite the creation of new styles. It was one of the first factory-made types of furniture, lending itself to this form of manufacture because of its

An example of Gothic-style needlepoint worked in cross-stitch on canvas. See page 141 for graph. The background is brown, the outline of each figure is rusty beige, and the two-color objects inside are alternating rows of rose and olive and orange and blue. The background around the objects is white. Photo: Philip L. Coltrain.

simple lines and simple scroll shapes. Joseph Meeks of New York, an
early manufacturer and wholesaler, advertised over thirty items in the
classical style in 1833. His advertisements stated that the furniture was
covered in silk or horsehair. In 1840 John Hall published *The Cabinet
Makers' Assistant*, which showed classical designs suitable for production in the factory rather than in the one-man shop.

Gothic revival furniture started in France in the late 1820s, but it
did not receive much attention in the United States for another ten years.
Then for the next forty years, though it was never widely popular, it
was made and sold. It is characterized by vertical lines and all the orna-

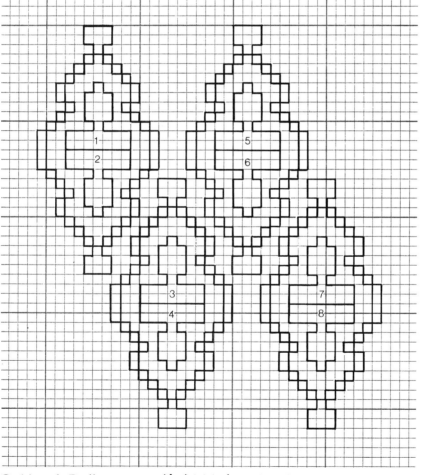

Gothic-style Berlin pattern, mid-nineteenth century.

Gothic chair, American.

mental features of Gothic design, lancets, cusps, and crockets. The rococo revival followed close on the heels of the Gothic and was accepted more widely by the American people. It had started in Europe in the 1830s but did not make its mark in the United States for another ten years. Called rococo revival by some and French Antique by others, the period produced two rather distinctive types of furniture, the balloon-back side chair and Belter furniture. The balloon-back chair has an oval gracefully perched on low uprights, an upholstered seat, and a modified cabriole leg. Its outline is one of soft curves and simple carved trim. By the 1850s it was one of the most popular styles sold. The typical needlework for a balloon-back chair was a nosegay of flowers with a plain background, but in later years anything that pleased the embroideress might be used, even striped designs.

Though the French revival started off with rococo, it was not the only import from that country. Louis Quatorze, Quinze, and Seize took their turns in the fancy of the American public and their decorators. By

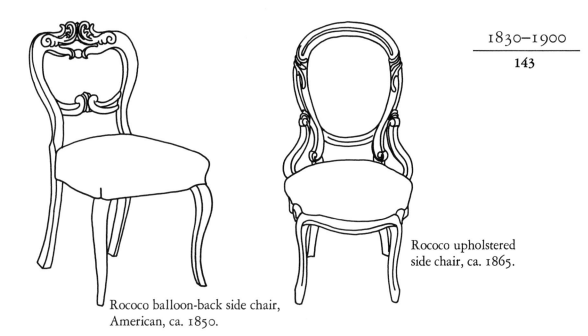

Rococo balloon-back side chair,
American, ca. 1850.

Rococo upholstered
side chair, ca. 1865.

the 1890s Louis Seize was clearly the favorite. None of these revivals
were for historical purists; they were American interpretations.

John Belter is the best-known manufacturer of rococo furniture,
and today his work is highly prized by museums and collectors. The

Rococo sofa, ca. 1860.

Rosewood chair in the rococo style with original needlepoint upholstery, ca. 1850. From the home of Ernest Fiedler and his wife, New York City. Courtesy of the Museum of the City of New York.

curves of Belter furniture are profusely embellished with carved flowers, foliage, and grapes. The carving extends like an enormous pierced ruff from the curved backs of chairs and sofas, undulating gracefully down to form a padded arm extending in a further curve of carved wood to the seat. The legs are always the same—low cabriole with a volute foot. Damask is the usual covering. Belter patented a laminating process in 1856 whereby thin sheets of wood, usually rosewood, were pressed together in curves. It produced a very strong curved back, suitable for pierced carving.

The Elizabethan revival was next. It reverted to vertical lines but continued the intricate, pierced carving of Belter's furniture. The legs and uprights were spirally turned on many pieces. The general outline was symmetrical, high-backed, and not very comfortable-looking. Elizabethan revival needlework seems more ordered than the textiles made

Pair of stools in the rococo
style, mahogany frames,
needlepoint and beaded
upholstery. Courtesy of the
Museum of the City of
New York.

Drawing-room sofa in the rococo revival style or the French style, as the
English called it. From *The Victorian Cabinet-Maker's Assistant*, Blackie
and Sons, originally printed in 1853. This illustrates the damask pattern the
firm thought appropriate for this style of sofa. Photo: Philip L. Coltrain.

Belter chair, ca. 1850s.

Damask pattern in white and orange with a background of deep crimson, described and illustrated in *The Crystal Palace Exhibition Illustrated Catalogue*, London, 1851. Manufactured by T. Ackroyd & Son of Halifax. Photo: Philip L. Coltrain.

at the same time. There is a tapestry-like quality to it, and more balance to the elements of design. Perhaps the symmetry of the back suggested a more ordered design to the embroiderer. The prie-dieu, which has a low seat and a high padded yoke, was a great favorite for covering with needlepoint upholstery. Combined flowers and strapwork was a typical design of this style.

The Renaissance revival followed the Elizabethan. It had started in France where it was called François I. The back of a Renaissance chair is shield-shaped with a small shield-like decoration carved at the crest of the back. The straight legs are vase-shaped. The Renaissance revival took on new vigor with the revised edition in 1878 of Charles Eastlake's *Hints on Household Taste in Furniture, Upholstery and Other Details.* It had been published first in England in 1868. Eastlake believed that art and practicality should be equal in furniture design. Furniture should be honestly and solidly built with no foolish fripperies. American manufacturers made their own interpretations of Eastlake's return to simplicity and his medieval-like designs, and then they tacked his name onto them. About all that remained were straight lines and incised designs. Other revivals included the New Greek (given to rolled-over backs and rather French lines otherwise), Turkish, Moorish, and Japanese. The final one was the Colonial revival, which resurrected all the early English styles.

One of the problems in identifying styles of the second half of the nineteenth century is that during the various revivals the American furniture makers followed their own interpretations of a stylized interpretation of the real thing. It was not unusual to add a detail from another style if it so pleased the maker. Furthermore, the revival styles were made and remade over such a long period of time that certain essential traits might be lost. The final revival, the Colonial revival, without any historical accuracy reproduced Chippendale chairs with a spoon back and klismos-backed chairs with cabriole legs. The only thing to do as far as

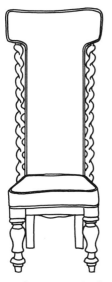

Elizabethan revival
prie-dieu, American.

Rococo-style armchair.

Elizabethan revival–style side chair, mahogany and rosewood. The needlepoint seat was worked by Mrs. Richard Van Wyck, née Catherine Bergen Johnson, who was married in 1851. Courtesy of the Museum of the City of New York.

Renaissance revival side chair, mahogany, with needlepoint seat, American, ca. 1856. Courtesy of the Brooklyn Museum, Dick S. Ramsey Fund.

needlework designs are concerned is to try to pick out the main recognizable feature of such a piece and work with that.

Andrew Jackson Downing in his *Architecture of Country Houses* (1850) called for velvet and other rich stuffs as appropriate materials for the Louis Quatorze revival. His description is apt. Damask, tabinet (a damask pattern with a watered background), brocatelle (a satin pattern against a twill background), and brocade would come under the "rich stuffs" category. They were some of the materials used for that period. The damask patterns used ranged from lace-like eighteenth-century patterns to repeats of fairly simple designs to extremely elaborate foliage

Walnut and mahogany side chair
with needlepoint upholstery,
American, ca. 1865. Courtesy of
the Brooklyn Museum, Gift
of John H. Livingston.

Sofa, American, ca. 1850–
1870. The needlepoint
depicts Mary and her lamb.
Courtesy of the Brooklyn
Museum, Bequest of Isabel
L. Whitney.

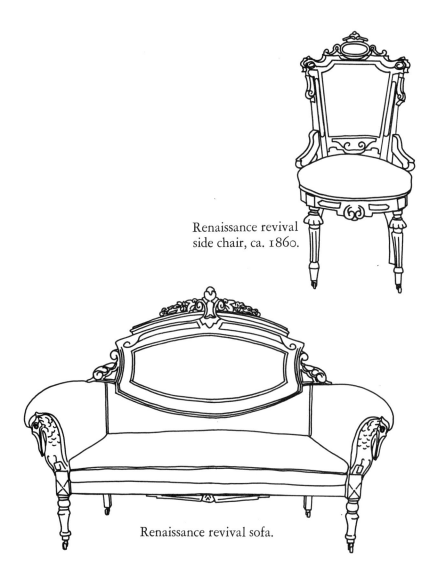

Renaissance revival
side chair, ca. 1860.

Renaissance revival sofa.

twining around trellises to stripes overlaid or combined with conventional damask patterns. The damasks were made of cotton and wool, wool, wool and silk, and silk and linen. Cotton prints were similar in the profusion of styles from which to choose. Flowers and foliage were by far the most popular subject matter, intricate in detail and profuse in growth. Flower patterns were either laid on top of another pattern, such as a

Upholstered side chair from the Fort Hunter Mansion House and Museum. Furnishings in the mansion date from 1775 to the 1880s. The custom of applying a strip of needlework up the seat and back of a tufted chair was not unusual in the 1870s and 1880s, nor was the heavy fringe. Courtesy of the Fort Hunter Mansion House and Museum, Harrisburg, Pennsylvania. Photo: courtesy of Laurence E. Lechleitner.

simple diaper design, or laid over fancy strapwork. Damask patterns were considered appropriate for all the revival styles. A tapestry-like material as well as plush was used on Renaissance revival chairs in the 1870s.

Tufting was used for all the revival styles except the Colonial revival, particularly if the covering was velvet or damask. Gimp, fancy tassels, and deep fringe were applied to chairs and stools of all styles. The corded fringe might be five or six inches deep and completely hide the legs of the chair.

As mentioned earlier, Berlin work was the chief form of embroidery used for upholstery. The early patterns were fairly open and simple whether landscape or floral. By the middle of the century, the floral patterns were quite dense and the figurative patterns quite detailed, going so far as to reproduce Scottish tartan kilts. By the 1870s the fashion turned to geometric strapwork in many colors. This type of design was

Seat and arm pads for late Victorian armchair, probably rococo in style. Courtesy of the Valentine Museum, Richmond, Virginia.

Back of the Victorian armchair. Wool cross-stitch on canvas. The background is black. Courtesy of the Valentine Museum, Richmond, Virginia.

WORK-BAG OR CHAIR-SEAT· PETERSON'S MAGAZINE, JANUARY, 1861.

Graphed needlepoint pattern included in color in the January 1861 issue of *Peterson's Magazine*. Photo: Philip L. Coltrain.

PETERSON'S MAGAZINE, FEBRUARY, 1861.

PATTERN FOR CHAIR SEAT IN BERLIN WORK.

Pattern for chair seat in color from February 1861 issue of *Peterson's Magazine.* Photo: Philip L. Coltrain.

used on Gothic and Renaissance revival furniture. Rococo and Elizabethan revival used floral patterns and fleur-de-lis-type repeats more. After the 1850s the design might not have anything to do with the style of the chair. A Gothic design full of crockets and lancets might grace a light, curvy balloon-back chair, or a Paisley design might be placed on the back of an Elizabethan revival chair. As the century progressed, the idea of "effect" superseded that of permanence. Inferior materials were used, and the ladies' magazines stressed the words *inexpensive* and *quick to work up.* Ugly stitchery trim was added to otherwise quite decent-looking Berlin work.

Needlepoint upholstery for stools and side chairs was often boxed whether the seat was round or square. The edges were trimmed with matching cording, sometimes made from the same wools as those used in the design. The design on the strip used for boxing did not necessarily have to match the design on the top.

There are no hard and fast rules on color for needlepoint in the second half of the nineteenth century. Rust and a peachy tan, as well as olive green and black, seem to have been favorites for backgrounds. Designs were often outlined in silk. The work was usually done on a

Ottoman from the Fort Hunter Mansion House and Museum, ca. 1875. Note the heavy cord couched in a wave pattern on the sides. Courtesy of the Fort Hunter Mansion House and Museum, Harrisburg, Pennsylvania. Photo: courtesy of Lawrence E. Lechleitner.

MAGASIN DES DEMOISELLES, 51, rue Laffitte

1850   SEMÉ POUR CHAISES VOLANTES

French needlepoint pattern
included in a ladies' magazine,
1880. Photo: Philip L. Coltrain.

Repeat mosaic-like pattern from
French ladies' magazine of the
1880s, suggested for a chair seat.
Photo: Philip L. Coltrain.

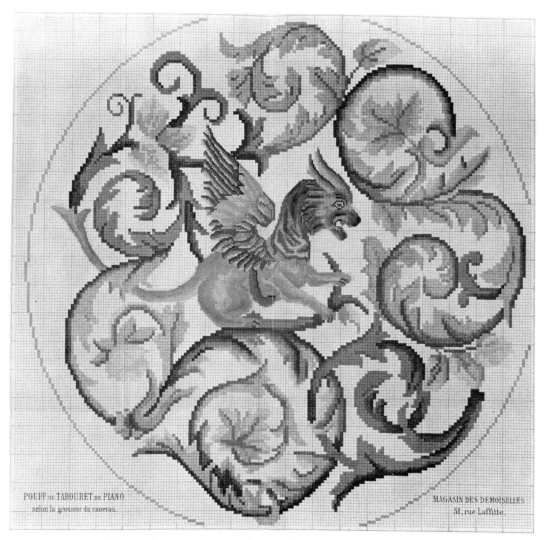

POUFF ou TABOURET de PIANO
selon la grosseur du canevas.

MAGASIN DES DEMOISELLES
51, rue Laffitte.

Pattern for a piano stool from a French ladies' magazine of the 1880s; the colors are pastel. Photo: Philip L. Coltrain.

two-thread canvas. The stitches used for Berlin work were at first just tent stitch (half cross-stitch) and cross-stitch. Gobelin and Smyrna cross-stitch were popular about 1835, and after them came the deluge of fancy stitches. By 1860 even arrangements of long stitches were being honored with a specific stitch name. It is interesting to note that most of the canvases still on their original chairs were worked in half cross-stitch or some kind of cross-stitch.

Beadwork, being a more tedious technique than half cross-stitch, was used for the subject matter of a canvas but rarely, if ever, for the background. Existing examples grace footstools and fire screens, though bead-

Seat for a prie-dieu from a French ladies' magazine of the 1880s. Photo: Philip L. Coltrain.

Stool top of beaded work with half cross-stitch background of green wool. The stool is gilded and dates from the second half of the nineteenth century. This very low stool is sometimes called a cricket stool. Courtesy of the Valentine Museum, Richmond, Virginia.

work was put on chairs too. At first colored beads were used. After the Civil War, silver, gray, bronze, white, black, and clear beads were the fashion. As the beads grew in size, the work diminished in good taste. Beadwork went out of style for furniture by the 1880s, but it continued in vogue for pincushions and small trifles into the twentieth century.

In the 1860s braidwork was the rage for trimming clothing and "trifles." It was used for cushion and footstool covers too. A stool cover was draped over a footstool like a tablecloth, not fitted like a slipcover.

Tassels trimmed the corners. Tape was stitched down on the cloth in looping patterns, and then herringbone stitch was embroidered on top of the tape. Flowers or Paisley shapes in cloth or felt were appliquéd in the center of the cover, and they too were then embroidered on and over. Flat tape was stitched onto muslin in geometric quilt-like patterns and then used for cushion covers.

In the 1880s Art Needlework supplanted Berlin work. It is best described as florid floral stitchery. The materials were either glossy silk floss on plush or drab "authentic" crewels on crash, depending on the effect desired. It was used for cushion covers, hangings, and clothing. Outline embroidery, using only the stem stitch and French knots, was another form of embroidery used for cushion covers. Designs were symmetrical.

Ombré silks were used by those ladies who did not feel capable of

Armchair, upholstered in blue velvet, American, late nineteenth century, in the Moorish style. Courtesy of the Brooklyn Museum, Gift of John D. Rockefeller, Jr.

shading their embroidered flowers and leaves. The silk in each skein was variegated in shade, a technique that actually started in the 1850s. Arrasene was a flat chenille-like thread, made in silk and in wool, used to embroider velvet, plush, and satin. It could be used in the needle along with wool to brighten the effect. When completed, the work was brushed with a soft brush to make all the fuzz of the thread stand up. It was mainly used with stem stitch and was popular in the late 1880s.

For the more elegant Louis Seize revival furniture, which was upholstered in satin, a contrasting color of silk might be used to embroider medallions for the seat and back. An arabesque frame might be worked to frame the owner's flowing monogram in the center of the back. Stem stitch and satin stitch were used. There is a strong possibility that this type of work was done professionally and not by loving hands at home.

Fancy painted chair, ca. 1890, with chair pad of cut velvet in imitation of embroidery, specifically cross-stitch. Photo originates from the Rose Studio in Providence, Rhode Island. Photo: Philip L. Coltrain.

Since the nineteenth century was such a period of revivals, there is little point in listing motifs. Just dip back into the previous centuries or go to the library and check out books on toleware patterns, William Morris and the Arts and Crafts Movement, the Crystal Palace Exhibition in 1851, *Godey's Lady's Book*, museum catalogs of textile collections, or any of the excellent picture books on Victorian life.

Stitches

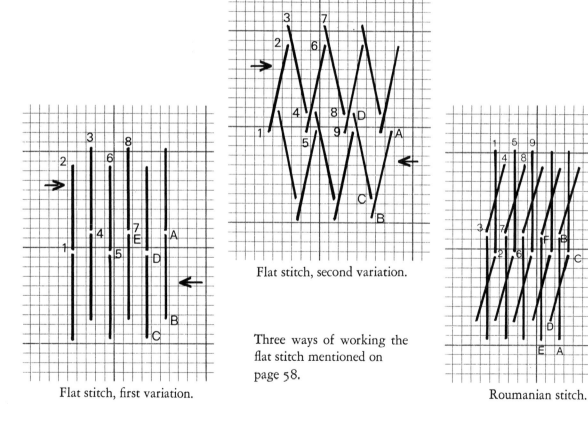

Flat stitch, first variation.

Flat stitch, second variation.

Three ways of working the flat stitch mentioned on page 58.

Roumanian stitch.

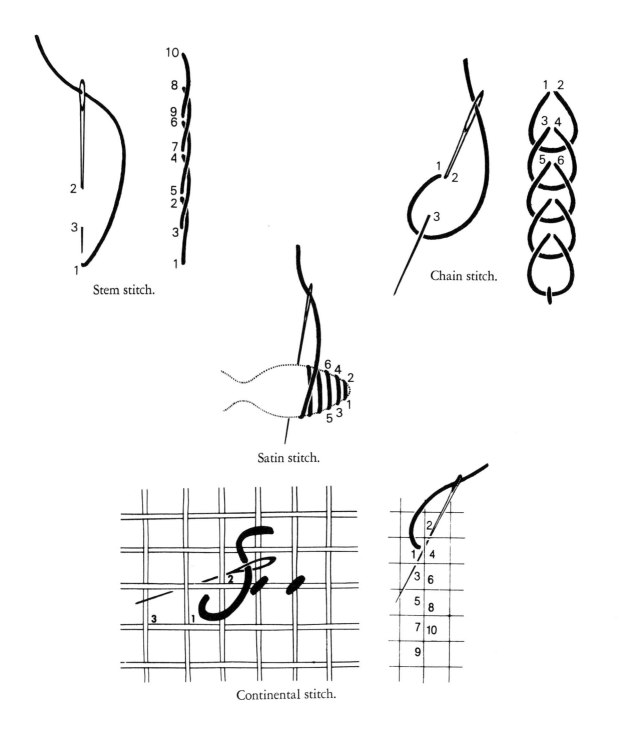

Stem stitch.

Chain stitch.

Satin stitch.

Continental stitch.

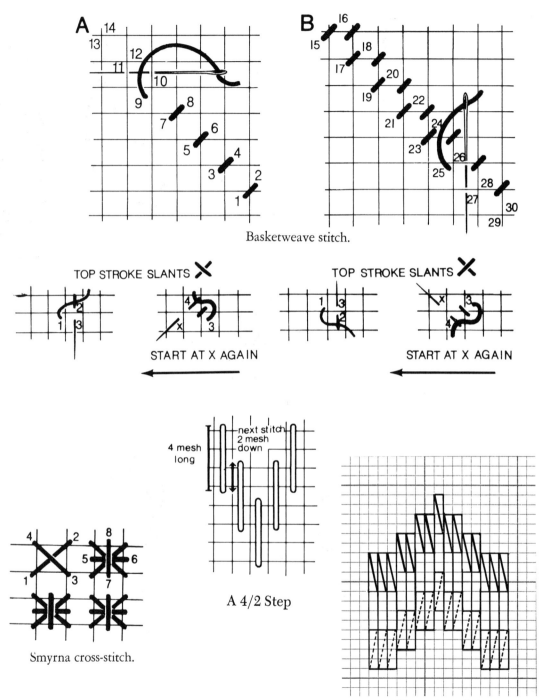

A

14
13
12
11
10
9 8
7 6
5 6
5 4
3 4
3 2
1 2

B

16
15 18
17 20
19 22
21 24
23 26
25 26
27 28
29 30

Basketweave stitch.

TOP STROKE SLANTS ✗

TOP STROKE SLANTS ✗

START AT X AGAIN

START AT X AGAIN

4 mesh long

next stitch 2 mesh down

A 4/2 Step

4 2
5 6
1 3
8
7

Smyrna cross-stitch.

Florentine stitch.

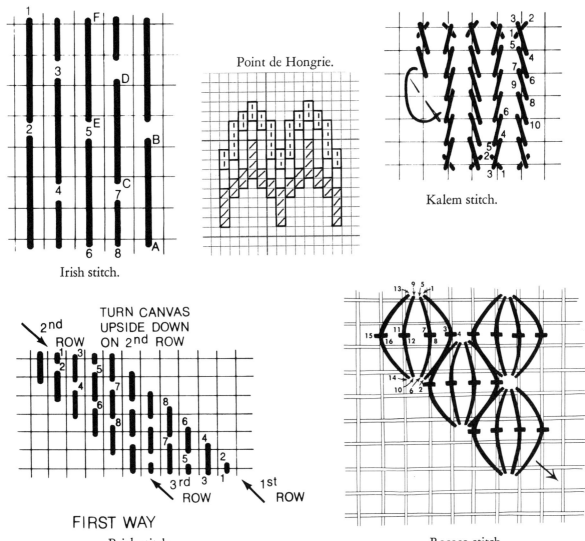

Irish stitch.

Point de Hongrie.

Kalem stitch.

TURN CANVAS
UPSIDE DOWN
ON 2nd ROW

2nd
ROW

3rd
ROW

1st
ROW

FIRST WAY

Brick stitch.

Rococo stitch.

BIBLIOGRAPHY

AMES, WINSLOW. *Prince Albert and Victorian Taste.* New York: The Viking Press, 1968.

ARONSON, JOSEPH. *The New Encyclopedia of Furniture.* New York: Crown Publishers, 1967.

BIENENSTOCK, N. I. *A History of American Furniture.* Furniture World—Furniture South, 1970.

BISHOP, ROBERT C. *Centuries and Styles of the American Chair.* New York: E. P. Dutton, 1972.

BISHOP, ROBERT. *Guide to American Antique Furniture.* New York: Galahad Books, 1973.

BOGER, LOUISE ADE. *The Complete Guide to Furniture Styles,* enlarged ed. New York: Charles Scribner's Sons, 1969.

BOGER, LOUISE ADE. *Furniture Past and Present.* New York: Doubleday, 1966.

BOORSCH, SUZANNE; JOHNSON, MARILYNN; and SCHWARTZ, MARVIN. *19th Century America: Furniture and Other Decorative Arts.* The Metropolitan Museum of Art. New York: New York Graphic Society, 1970.

BRIDGEMAN, HARRIET, and DRURY, ELIZABETH, eds. *The Encyclopedia of Victoriana.* New York: Macmillan, 1975.

BUSH, FLORENCE GUILD, and WELBOURNE, FRANCES. *Design: Its Fundamentals and Applications.* Boston: Little, Brown, 1937.

CESCINSKY, HERBERT. *English Furniture: From Gothic to Sheraton.* New York: Dover Publications, 1968.

167

CESCINSKY, HERBERT, and HUNTER, GEORGE LELAND. *English and American Furniture.* New York: Garden City Publishing Co., 1929.

CHIPPENDALE, THOMAS. *The Gentleman & Cabinet-Maker's Director.* Reprint of the 3rd ed., 1762. New York: Dover Publications, 1966.

CHRISTIE, ARCHIBALD H. *Pattern Design*, 2nd ed. New York: Dover Publications, 1969.

COMSTOCK, HELEN. *American Furniture.* New York: Bonanza Books, 1962.

CONSTANTINO, RUTH T. *How to Know French Antiques.* New York: Clarkson N. Potter, 1961.

CORNELIUS, CHARLES O. *Early American Furniture.* New York: The Century Co., 1926.

CRAIG, JAMES H. *The Arts & Crafts in North Carolina.* Winston-Salem, N.C.: The Museum of Early Southern Decorative Arts, Old Salem, Inc., 1965.

The Crystal Palace Exhibition Illustrated Catalogue. London, 1851. Reprinted New York: Dover Publications, 1970.

DAVIDSON, MARSHALL B., and *American Heritage* EDITORS. *The American Heritage History of Colonial Antiques.* New York: American Heritage Publishing Co., 1968.

DAVIS, MILDRED. *The Art of Crewel Embroidery.* New York: Crown Publishers, 1962.

DIGBY, GEORGE WINGFIELD. *Elizabethan Embroidery.* New York: Thomas Yoseloff, Publisher, 1963.

DOW, GEORGE FRANCIS. *The Arts & Crafts in New England, 1704–1755.* Topsfield, Mass.: The Wayside Press, 1927.

DOWNING, A. J. *Furniture for the Victorian Home: The Architecture of Country Houses.* Reprinted New York: American Life Foundation, 1968.

DOWNS, JOSEPH. *American Furniture: Queen Anne and Chippendale Periods.* New York: Macmillan, 1952.

EASTLAKE, CHARLES L. *Hints on Household Taste in Furniture, Upholstery and other Details*, 1875. Reprinted New York: Dover Publications, 1969.

EDWARDS, RALPH, and RAMSEY, L. G. G., eds. *The Connoisseur Guides to the Houses, Furnishing and Chattels of the Classic Periods*, vols. I–IV. New York: Reynal & Co.

EHRESMAN, JULIA, ed. *The Pocket Dictionary of Art Terms.* Boston: New York Graphic Society, 1971.

FITZ-GERALD, DESMOND, ed. *Georgian Furniture—Victoria and Albert Museum.* London: Her Majesty's Stationery Office, 1969.

FOWLER, JOHN, and CORNFORTH, JOHN. *English Decoration in the 18th Century.* Princeton, N.J.: The Pyne Press, 1974.

GOTTESMAN, RITA SUSSWEIN. *The Arts and Crafts in New York, 1726–1776.* New York: Printed for the New-York Historical Society by J. J. Little and Ives Co., 1938.

GOWANS, ALAN. *Images of American Living: Four Centuries of Architecture and Furniture as Cultural Expression.* New York: Harper & Row, 1964.

HIND, ARTHUR M. *A History of Engraving & Etching.* New York: Dover Publications, 1963.

HOLLOWAY, EDWARD STRATTON. *The Practical Book of American Furniture and Decoration.* Philadelphia: J. B. Lippincott, 1937.

HOWE, MARGERY BURNHAM. *Deerfield Embroidery.* New York: Charles Scribner's Sons, 1976.

IRWIN, JOHN, and BRETT, KATHARINE B. *Origins of Chintz.* London: Her Majesty's Stationery Office, 1970.

JOY, EDWARD T., and WILLS, GEOFFREY. *The Collector's Book of English Antiques.* New York: A. S. Barnes, 1964.

KENWORTHY-BROWNE, JOHN. *Chippendale and His Contemporaries.* London: Orbis Publishing, 1971.

KENWORTHY-BROWNE, JOHN, and MOLESWORTH, H. D. *Three Centuries of Furniture.* New York: The Viking Press, 1969.

KIRK, JOHN T. *American Chairs: Queen Anne and Chippendale.* New York: Alfred A. Knopf, 1972.

LAVER, JAMES. *Victoriana.* New York: Hawthorne Books, 1967.

LICHTEN, FRANCES. *Decorative Art of Victoria's Era.* New York: Charles Scribner's Sons, 1950.

LITTLE, FRANCES. *Early American Textiles.* New York: The Century Co., 1931.

LOCKWOOD, LUKE VINCENT. *Colonial Furniture in America,* vols. I–II. New York: Charles Scribner's Sons, 1926.

MACQUOID, PERCY. *A History of English Furniture,* vols. I–IV. New York:

Dover Publications, 1972. (Originally published London: Lawrence & Bullen, 1904.)

MANWARING, ROBERT. *The Cabinet and Chair-Maker's Real Friend and Companion*, 1765. Reprinted London: John Tiranti, 1947.

MAYER, CHRISTINA CHARLOTTE. *Masterpieces of Western Textiles from the Art Institute of Chicago*. Chicago: Art Institute of Chicago, 1969.

MAYER, RALPH. *A Dictionary of Art and Techniques*. New York: Thomas Y. Crowell, 1969.

MILLER, EDGAR G. *American Antique Furniture*, 1937. Reprinted (2 volumes in one) New York: Dover Publications, 1966.

MONTGOMERY, CHARLES F. *American Furniture: The Federal Period*. New York: The Viking Press, 1966.

MONTGOMERY, FLORENCE M. *Printed Textiles, English and American Cottons and Linens*, 1700–1850. New York: The Viking Press, 1970.

MOORE, N. HUDSON. *The Olde Furniture Book*. New York: Tudor Publishing Co., 1903.

MORSE, FRANCES CLARY. *Furniture of the Olden Time*. New York: Macmillan, 1903.

OTTO, CELIA JACKSON. *American Furniture of the Nineteenth Century*. New York: The Viking Press, 1965.

PEGLER, MARTIN. *The Dictionary of Interior Design*. New York: Bonanza Books, 1966.

PERGOLESI, MICHELANGELO. *Classical Ornaments of the Eighteenth Century*. New York: Dover Publications, 1970.

PETERSON, HAROLD L. *Americans at Home: From the Colonists to the Late Victorians*. New York: Charles Scribner's Sons, 1971.

Peterson's Magazine, January–December 1861. Philadelphia, Pa.

PRIME, ALFRED COXE, ed. *The Arts & Crafts in Philadelphia, Maryland, and South Carolina, 1721–1755*. The Walpole Society, 1929.

PRIME, ALFRED COXE, ed. *The Arts & Crafts in Philadelphia, Maryland, and South Carolina, 1786–1800*. The Walpole Society, 1932.

REMINGTON, PRESTON. *English Domestic Needlework of the XVI, XVII and XVIII Centuries*. New York: Metropolitan Museum of Art, 1945.

SACK, ALBERT. *Fine Points of Furniture*. New York: Crown Publishers, 1950.

SEALE, WILLIAM, *The Tasteful Interlude: American Interiors through the Camera's Eye*. New York: Praeger Publishers, 1975.

SHERATON, THOMAS. *The Cabinet-Maker and Upholsterer's Drawing-Book*. New York: Dover Publications, 1972.

SINGLETON, ESTHER. *The Furniture of Our Forefathers*. New York: Benjamin Blom, 1970.

SMITH, HELEN EVERTSON. *Colonial Days and Ways*. New York: The Century Co., 1900.

SNOOK, BARBARA. *Florentine Embroidery*. New York: Charles Scribner's Sons, 1967.

STRANGE, THOMAS ARTHUR. *French Interiors, Furniture, Decoration, Woodwork & Allied Arts*. New York: Bonanza Books, 1968.

SWAN, SUSAN BURROWS, and LANDON, MARY TAYLOR. *American Crewelwork*. New York: Macmillan, 1970.

SWEENEY, JOHN A. H. *Winterthur Illustrated*. New York: Chanticleer Press, 1963.

VERLAT, PIERRE. *French Cabinetmakers of the Eighteenth Century*. New York: Hachette, 1965.

VICTORIA AND ALBERT MUSEUM. *English Chairs*. London: Her Majesty's Stationery Office, 1970.

VICTORIA AND ALBERT MUSEUM. *The Franco-British Exhibition of Textiles, 1921*. London: Her Majesty's Stationery Office, 1922.

The Victorian Cabinet-Makers' Assistant. Blackie and Sons, 1853. Reprinted New York: Dover Publications, 1970.

WARREN, DAVID B. *American Furniture, Paintings and Silver from the Bayou Bend Collection*. Houston: The Museum of Fine Arts, 1975.

WAY, NELSON E., and STAPLETON, CONSTANCE. *Antiques Don't Lie*. New York: Doubleday, 1975.

WHITTON, SHERRILL. *Elements of Interior Decoration*, rev. and enlarged ed. New York: J. B. Lippincott, 1944.

WILSON, ERICA. *Crewel Embroidery*. New York: Charles Scribner's Sons, 1963.

WINCHESTER, ALICE, ed. *The Antiques Treasury of Furniture and the Decorative Arts*. New York: Galahad Books, 1977.

WOODFORDE, JOHN. *The Observer's Book of Furniture*. New York: Charles Scribner's Sons, 1977.

The Young Ladies' Journal: Complete Guide to the Work-table. London: E. Harrison, Merton House, 1885.

INDEX